REPRESENTATIVE WOMEN

General Editor: Francis Birrell

MARY SHELLEY

REPRESENTATIVE WOMEN

First Volumes :

Mary
Shelley

MARY SHELLEY

BY

RICHARD CHURCH

THE FOLCROFT PRESS, INC.
FOLCROFT, PA.

First Published 1928

Reprinted 1969

MARY SHELLEY

BY

RICHARD CHURCH

GERALD HOWE LTD
23 SOHO SQUARE
LONDON

*The frontispiece portrait
drawn by* J. GOWER PARKS
from contemporary sources

PRINTED IN GREAT BRITAIN 1928

TO

ROGER INGPEN

MARY SHELLEY
(1797–1851)

I

THERE are human beings who are singled out as the
particular sport of the gods. Mary Shelley was one of them.
She had every endowment except good fortune. Beauty,
charm, a keen intellect, and even a touch of genius ; all
these were given her : but from the moment of her birth to
within a few years of her death, she was cruelly tortured by
circumstance. The mere facts and accidents of life betrayed
her at every turn. But only the most uncharitable of her
friends could say that life defeated her. We shall see the
equanimity and unexampled meekness with which she bore
these bludgeonings of fate, and how her 'singularly bold,
somewhat imperious, and active mind '—as her famous
father described her—learned to submit itself with a minimum
of resentment to fate's cruel disciplinary knocks.

Her disposition had a rich and conflicting inheritance. She
was born of both fire and water, and in the early years of her
life the conflict of these two elements, aggravated by the
intrusion of the third element of air—her husband—gave her
no peace of mind. And, indeed, it reverberated within her
long after strife had ceased with the triumph of water, the
philosophic calm of Godwin.

Her father, William Godwin, was born in 1756 at Wisbech
near Cambridge. His parents were comfortable provincial

folk, his father being a dissenting minister with a strong
Calvinistic bias. William was accordingly brought up strictly,
in an atmosphere of sectarian discipline and self-examination.
He was given such pleasant reading as *An Account of the
Pious Deaths of many Godly Children.* It is said that once,
on a Sunday, he picked up a stray cat and hugged it in
his arms. This touch of the natural samaritan was severely
censured by his father as an act of levity unfit for the
Sabbath.

Everything, in short, tended to make a little prig of Godwin, and with some misgivings we find him, as a child,
preaching sermons on Sunday afternoons to the servants in the
kitchen. By the age of eight he had read all through the
Bible. As he grew older he became more strait than his
preceptors, joining a special sect of north-country evangelists
who called themselves Sandemanians, and followed one John
Glas, whom Godwin afterwards described as 'a celebrated
apostle who, after Calvin had damned ninety-nine in a hundred
of mankind, has contrived a scheme for damning ninety-nine
in a hundred of the followers of Calvin.'

It was inevitable that the young Godwin became a minister,
and he followed this calling at various places in the Midlands.
At one of them, Stowmarket, he met Joseph Fawset, an
ardent republican and advocate of the sanctity of Reason.
The influence of this man worked like magic on the un-
developed personality of the righteous young preacher.
Godwin suddenly found himself, and began rapidly to develop
his latent power. He swallowed the French Encyclopædists
—a popular diet for the young at that time—and came to
London full of strength and purpose, to convince mankind
that in syllogisms lay salvation, and that only a golden chain
of logic was needed to force the lion of ownership to lie down
with the lamb of servitude.

In London he set to work as a 'heavy' journalist,
writing historical sketches for *The Annual Register*. In
addition to this work he published a *Life of Lord Chatham*

and a collection of sermons. The latter, perhaps, first in-
dicated the special bent of his mind. He ventured on an
arraignment of the popular conception of God as a tyrant,
and laid down thereby the foundation of his theory of
'political justice.' To our cynical generation this phrase is
a contradiction in terms, for we see no possibility of connect-
ing politics with justice, recognizing modern statecraft to
have degenerated into a mere manipulation of economic
and financial forces that tends only to annihilate individual
freedom and the sanctity of human personality. Godwin,
however, was like us inasmuch as he recognized this danger,
and indeed his leanings towards a conscious and responsible
anarchy were curiously modern. He voices many of our
aspirations towards a paradoxical society that is a sort of
decentralised unit, a kind of federation of parishes wherein the
individual can flourish unmenaced by too rigid an economic
machine.

In his famous work, *The Inquiry concerning Political
Justice*, published in 1793, he clearly stated his belief that
'government by its very nature counteracts the improvement
of original mind.' In this we shall see that the rebellious
Protestantism of his religious youth was now seeking political
expression in the form of idealistic anarchy, which was the
spirit of the French Revolution and the life-breath of the
Romantic Movement. He was, as Hazlitt claimed for him,
a true expression of his own times. He believed in the innate
virtue of the human soul, and that tragedy and vice are the
mechanical results of evil environment. In the weapon of
Reason, man possessed an unfailing defence against the
external enemy. Logic was the only force whose laws were
inviolable, and consequently man must live solely within its
bounds, for beyond them were the blind powers of passion,
cowardice, and tyranny.

This doctrine of 'self-possession' is preached by every
religious genius, from Buddha, Christ, and Plato downwards.
But the Lucifer who is latent in all such supreme beings rode

uppermost in Godwin. The 'guiding rational sanity' of
Plato's political man was the nearest approach to Godwin's
ideal, but Plato's conception was infinitely greater and more
complete because it was cognisant of an external reservoir
of wisdom from which the individual was fed. He made the
unit conform to the type ; and in this inspiration of humility
gave a living and organic rightness to his political theory.
But Godwin was too proud to be so large. Logic to him was
a self-generated force ; and the man who lived by it was a
proud star that looked to no central luminary.

Godwin followed up his *Political Justice* with a novel,
Caleb Williams. As a result of these two books he became
a literary and philosophic lion, and for some years he
sat in state, a sort of Dr Johnson, but without Johnson's
emotional perturbations. Emotion and personal possessions
he regarded as fetters, tying the individual to external em-
barrassments.

He was destined, however, to be victimised by both these
forces. Two years later he met the famous Mary Wollstonecraft, and his pride received its first tumble. He had
looked upon marriage as one of the worst of those legal
fetters which he spent his life in denouncing. But he had
to marry Mary, and shamefacedly to conceal his marriage for
a time.

Mary Wollstonecraft is a name which still stirs the heart
with images of nobility. She stands as a monument of pure
feeling and candour. Rich-hearted and impulsive, she flashed
on the sober stream of Godwin's personality like a sunset
fire along a smooth river. His pride never afterwards had
quite the same integrity and self-continence.

She was born at Hoxton in 1759, of an Irish mother and
a drunkard father. Her childhood, with that of her sisters,
was one of misery. She saw all the womankind in her small
world the slaves of an irresolute male despot. She saw her
mother beaten by him. The shame and the injustice rankled
in the girl's heart, and woke her to an early realization of

purpose. Her mother died when she was twenty-one, and after her father's second marriage, she left home with her two sisters, all intending to earn their own living—a sign of abnormal independence in those days. Her next acquaintance with male humanity was through her sister Eliza, who made a disastrous marriage. The legal separation which followed this resulted in the sisters setting up a school, with Fanny Blood, Mary's intimate friend and a girl of much culture. Godwin records that during this period of 'school-marming,' she met the great Dr Johnson, who encouraged her by his kindness. Neither Boswell, nor Fanny Burney, nor Mrs Thrale, however, so much as mention her name. Meanwhile Fanny Blood, who had been a guide and solace to the lonely girl, married a merchant and went away to Lisbon. This loss was followed by further trouble for Mary. The school failed, and her health broke down. Fanny Blood then invited her out to Lisbon, to act as nurse during the coming confinement. This event only plunged Mary into further grief, for her friend died in child-birth.

About this time she made her first essay in authorship, with a pamphlet on *Thoughts on the Education of Daughters*. She followed this with hackwork for a city bookseller, which enabled her to keep her head above water while she was writing the book which made her famous, the *Vindication of the Rights of Woman*.

All that she demanded for women was that they should be regarded seriously, educated equally with men as responsible members of society, and given opportunity to justify that equality by competing with men in the business and professional worlds. She also pleaded for equality in marriage and custody of children, and for a paternal responsibility in the maintenance of illegitimate children.

Following her success, and burning with the fire of her expressed ideas, she went to France in 1792 to watch the birth of freedom there. Alas, she herself fell into slavery, betrayed by her own spiritual generosity. The year following her arrival in Paris, she met the American, Gilbert Imlay, and fell deeply in love with him. He responded by utilising her for his pleasure and his business. She became his lover, and his commercial traveller. As he grew tired of her in the former rôle, she became relegated more and more to the latter. The result was a cruel immolation of herself. She tried again and again to win him back, and for a short time after the birth of her child she succeeded. The happiness did not last long, for she soon discovered that even while they were living as man and wife he was unfaithful to her. It all ended by her attempting to drown herself in the river at Putney. This frantic deed seemed to act as a cathartic for the unhappy passion which for over two years had wasted her. She then settled in London with her baby, who was named after the dead Fanny.

There followed a short period of real happiness, for in 1796 she met Godwin. Their acquaintance was ripened by mutual respect into a deep friendship that finally swept aside all their shared theories as to the contemptibility of marriage. In March 1797 they married secretly, and each kept a separate menage as a sort of sop to their principles. Godwin, however, crumbled fast, for passion, this new thing in his life, took tighter and tighter hold, heart and brain. The fact that he was to have a child by this wonderful flame-haired woman filled him with a bewildering excitement. He wrote to her as much as four times a day. Mary, however, wiser by her past experience, held herself in check, especially against the somewhat overbearing logical masculinity of her husband. On a point of order, as it were, we find her resentful that he expected her, during some domestic need, to negotiate with a plumber, regarding the delegation to her of this mundane matter as a hint of her intellectual inferiority. Godwin, on the other hand, became emotionally expansive and even took to little Fanny, and for the rest of her life treated her as his own child.

At last Mary's time came. On August 30th 1797, she

gave birth to another daughter, Mary. Within a few hours
dangerous complications set in, and after ten days of agony
for herself and her husband, she died, leaving the new-born
infant, and her little girl of three, in the hands of the middle-
aged and bachelor-minded rationalist.

A PHILOSOPHER, A FOOL, AND A HOUSE-
HOLD

W O M E N friends, moved by the pathos of Godwin's hopeless situation, came to the rescue. Amongst them was a Mrs
Reveley, more familiar to us as Maria Gisborne, a gentle,
sane woman, who later was to be a good, because pacific
friend to Mary and Shelley. Godwin moved into the house
of his late wife, in Somers Town, and imported a housekeeper
and a wet nurse. The latter revolted Godwin by her mam-
malian emphasis, while the former terrified him by her
obvious designs upon his unhappy freedom. More and more
he realized his loss, and the vivid and compulsive influence
of domestic and worldly events into the life of the mind.
Shortly after Mary Wollstonecraft's death, we find him
writing :

‘ The poor children! I am myself totally unfitted to
educate them. The scepticism which perhaps sometimes
leads me right in matters of speculation is torment to me
when I would attempt to direct the infant mind. I am the
most unfit person for this office ; she was the best qualified
in the world. What a change ! The loss of the children
is less remediless than mine. You can understand the
difference.’

He struggled along for four years, occasionally imploring
one and then another of his women friends to marry him.
But his reasons for and methods of proposing were sufficiently
calculated and detached to ensure refusal. In 1799 Mrs

Reveley lost her husband, and Godwin allowed only a month to pass before he suggested that she should legalize her care for his children. She accentuated the mortification of her refusal by accepting Gisborne, a worthy man but a dull dog.

Like so many people who are out for a bargain, Godwin finally looked nearest home. He married his next-door neighbour, a widow named Mrs Clairmont, who had a boy and girl of her own. These were Charles, about seven years old, and Jane, a little dark irresponsible waif of four ; mischievous, but unfortunately for the people she tormented, always pardonable.

Mrs Clairmont was quite a new element in the rarefied atmosphere of the Godwin circle. Its gentle, theoretical, genuinely philosophic nature was torn to shreds ; for this good woman was a philistine of the worst kind. She was intelligent, dogmatic, know-all, righteous, and infernally noisy and hot-tempered. If she disagreed with people she ' blew them up,' completely oblivious of any sensitive nervous organism which they might possess. As this last is a common possession of genuine thinkers and people of real and creative intuition, such as Godwin and his two girls, it can be imagined what havoc this good lady wrought. She was more like an orphanage or institute than a woman. She compelled, she managed. The house became tidy in the wrong sort of way. One feels that sweepings and turnings-out loomed larger than peace of mind or fruitful talk. Discussion gave place to argument ; abstractions became personalities. In short, in her foolish, good-natured way she ' gave them hell.'

The new wife did not help Godwin to develop the belated emotional sensibility which Mary Wollstonecraft had awakened in him. Out of nervous self-defence, he had now to harden himself again, and repel vehemence with self-assertive vanity. He in his turn became somewhat heavy-handed, and thereby accentuated an ingrained weakness. The lustre of his fame became a little tarnished, and many of the more illustrious frequenters of his company departed. However, even the formidable Mrs Godwin could not banish the most intimate of Godwin's old associates, who recognized his true value, and the heroic and even prophetic quality of his mind.

In consequence, the sombre childhood of Mary Wollstonecraft's daughters was frequently cheered by inspired company. Coleridge, whose lofty genius was to influence their father so far as almost to kindle in him the saving grace of imagination, often came to the house. One night he proposed to read *The Ancient Mariner*, and the two girls hid themselves behind a sofa in order to hear the great poet mouthing his work with that magical voice of his. Their stepmother found them, unfortunately, and was for sending them off to bed. It would have been useless for them to plead that they longed to share the spiritual treat. To her, no doubt, it was just an eccentric event, common enough amongst these odd impractical people whom it was her lot to shepherd. Coleridge, however, pleaded for the children, and even Mrs Godwin could not resist the hypnotic persuasion of that voice.

Charles Lamb, too, came with his gift of whimsicality, a quality delightful to children. One night, at dinner, he blew out the candle, caught up the cold leg of mutton from the table and placed it in the hand of one of the guests. On the candle being relit, he cried out, ' Oh Martin! Martin! I should never have thought it of you! ' In another impulsive moment, he carried off a cruet, for which Mrs Godwin hunted in vain. Next day he walked quietly in as usual, and during conversation with the assembled family pulled the cruet from his pocket, replaced it on the table, and continued his stuttering talk as though he had done no more than take a pinch of snuff.

Such people, seasoning their more impressive influence with these charming incidents, were an inspiring school for the children. In addition, Godwin himself, with his magnifi-

cent mind and integrity, lifted them out of the ordinary rut
of domestic monotony. They talked with him, and heard
him discourse to the constant stream of young disciples who
came to the house. They went with him to lectures and
to the theatre. He even wrote books for them, an enterprise
which Mrs Godwin took up and placed on a commercial
footing. She persuaded her husband to set up as a publisher
of children's books, and they opened an establishment for
that purpose in Skinner Street, Holborn. Godwin adopted
the name of ' Baldwin,' thinking that his own reputation
as a free-thinker would not be a business asset for the firm.
The only book of note issued from Skinner Street was the
Tales from Shakespeare of the Lambs. The wrong-headed-
ness of Mrs Godwin and the abstraction of her husband
were not the best of capital for a business which was to help
the family out of its financial difficulties. There were now
five children, for Mrs Godwin had produced a son, William,
a rather unnoticeable little boy who grew up into a talented
young fellow, became a Parliamentary reporter, wrote a
novel, married, and died of cholera before he was thirty.
His death was a heavy blow to the parents, coming as it did
in their old age, after they had been bowed by so many
domestic tragedies and troubles. ·

The publishing business became only another mouth to
feed, and for the rest of his life Godwin lived on the edge of
ruin, postponing the inevitable bankruptcy only by borrow-
ings from his friends and giving promissory notes. Fortun-
ately, there were long periods of relief from this Bohemian
atmosphere of penury, philosophy, and muddle. Excursions
to the country gave Mary opportunity for fertile solitude.
In 1811, when she was fourteen, a slight trouble in the nerves
of her arm caused her parents to send her to Ramsgate.
There she stayed six months, coming home in December
quite robust again.

About this time the son Charles Clairmont went to work
in Edinburgh, and made the acquaintance of a family named

Baxter. The father was a methodical business man with a
large heart and a Scottish flair for metaphysics. He had long
admired Godwin's work and had known him personally
since 1809. Seeing that Mary was beginning to wilt in the
stuffy air of Skinner Street, Baxter invited her to come and
stay under the care of his wife and daughters for an indefinite
period. Accordingly she sailed for Dundee in June 1812.
Her going was both an anxiety and a relief for her father.
He was a man who found it difficult to get into an intimate
relationship with another human being, for he seemed to lack
that feminine touch, that wisp of intuition, which brings
more comprehension and fellow-feeling than the most
Socratic of arguments. He had very little compassion, and his
conscience made him regret his deficiency. The letter
which he wrote to Baxter is very tender where he touches
on these sore points : ' The old proverb says, " He is a
wise father who knows his own child," and I feel the justice
of the apothegm on the present occasion. There never can
be a perfect equality between father and child, and if he has
other objects and avocations to fill up the greater part of
his time, the ordinary resource is for him to proclaim his
wishes and commands in a way somewhat sententious and
authoritative, and occasionally to utter his censures with
seriousness and emphasis. It can, therefore, seldom happen
that he is the confidant of his child, or that the child does
not feel some degree of awe or restraint in intercourse with
him. I am not, therefore, a perfect judge of Mary's character.
I believe that she has nothing of what is commonly called
vices, and that she has considerable talent.'

One feels that he must often have smarted under the
eloquent reproaches of Mary's grey eyes, as they gazed at
him from under the clear, intellectual brow. Later in the
letter, he adds : ' I am anxious that she should be brought
up like a philosopher, even like a cynic. It will add greatly
to the strength and worth of her character. I wish too that
she should be *excited* to industry. She has occasionally

great perseverence, but occasionally, too, she shows great need to be roused.'

Here is an opportunity to compare her with Fanny Imlay, her half-sister. Mary possessed not a little of Godwin's aloofness and detachment, but dear, kind Fanny was all warmth and domestic friendliness. She was a busy soul, practical and helpful, supplying the motherliness and peace-making qualities which Mrs Godwin so sadly lacked. She was devoted to Godwin, to Mary, and to the memory of her mother ; and though at this time she knew nothing of the circumstances of her birth, there was a reflective, somewhat sober vein in her character as though her soul was acquainted with the agonies of mind which her mother, heavy in heart and womb, suffered before her birth.

Godwin compared the two girls thus : ' My own daughter is considerably superior in capacity to the one her mother had before. Fanny, the eldest, is of a quiet, modest, unshowy disposition, somewhat given to indolence, which is her greatest fault, but sober, observing, peculiarly clear and dis-tinct in the faculty of memory, and disposed to exercise her own thoughts and follow her own judgment. Mary, my daughter, is the reverse of her in many particulars. She is singularly bold, somewhat imperious, and active of mind. Her desire of knowledge is great, and her perseverance in everything she undertakes almost invincible. My own daughter is, I believe, very pretty. Fanny is by no means handsome, but, in general, prepossessing.'

Mary remained for five months with the Baxters at Dundee. It was another world for her ; one of normal domesticity, happy girlhood companionship, and open-air life. She made an intimate friend of Isabella Baxter, and was also on good terms with an elder sister Christy, who came back with her to London on a return visit. The day after that return they met a young couple of Godwin's admirers, named Mr and Mrs Shelley, and Christy Baxter (who lived to a great age and was full of reminiscences)

recalls Harriet Shelley's remarkable beauty, her brilliant
complexion and lovely hair, and her purple satin dress.
She also remembered how attentive Shelley was to his wife.
Nothing further was thought of the incident, and the next
two years were spent by Mary in dividing her time between
Skinner Street and Dundee. During that period she
developed from a child into a maiden—and a very interesting
one. Her attraction was different from that of her more
independent, fierce-hearted mother, with fire in hair and
eyes. She had not the same full-blossom quality. In her,
all seemed toned down by the severe intellectual training
which she had undergone almost from birth. She was a more
scholarly type than her mother, and accordingly more sub-
missive. We hear of her ' well-shaped head and intellectual
brow, her fine fair hair and liquid hazel eyes, and a skin and
complexion of singular whiteness and purity; a beauty of
a rare and refined type. She was somewhat below the medium
height ; very graceful with drooping shoulders and swan-like
throat. The serene eloquent eyes contrasted with a small
mouth, indicative of a certain reserve of temperament, which,
in fact, always distinguished her, and beneath which those who
did not know her might not have suspected her vigour of intellect and fearlessness of thought.' The singular power of the
rather mournful concentrated gaze of her large grey-to-hazel
eyes is commented on by many people at all periods of her life.
   She was a girl perhaps too richly endowed and educated.
The long holidays at Dundee were the only truly peaceful
and fallow parts in her life. All the rest had been spent in
a forcing-house. On the one hand was the premature intellectual and moral emancipation due to her father's tireless
example and teaching. With him and his friends she shared
in the most advanced thought of the age. She met giants who
were a law unto themselves, and who strode through the
etiquette and conventions of social life without a qualm.
Even the most emancipated parents would admit that such
preceptors were dangerous for an ardent, inexperienced girl.

On the other hand, we must realize that after her return from the happy Baxter home, where quiet, method, and sufficient intelligence were the order of the day, it was a shock for her to return to Skinner Street to resume her part in that ill-assorted household. Constant noise, opposed to the emphasized calm of Godwin, provided an incessant nervous irritant. The various types of character of the six people comprising the household were too severely contrasted to make for harmony. There was Mrs Godwin forming one spiritual pole, toward which graduated, while violently rebelling, her own two children. Jane, or as she afterwards called herself, Claire, was a violent, erratic young egoist, wantonly subjecting herself to fits of self-hypnotism out of pure desire for excitement and sensation. She was too self-interested and intelligent to believe in her own hysteria, and retained it purely as an instrument for getting her own way. One can imagine the sordid bickerings, outbursts of temper, strained relations, and veiled hostilities which charged the home with heaviness and storm; an atmosphere stifling to the mind of such a girl as Mary. To her young and intolerant idealism, there was no excuse for these people, and she looked upon her sister Fanny as being treacherous to the best things of life. For Fanny was interested more in people than ideas; she stood alone, and somewhat inscrutable, thinking her own very independent thoughts that fitted neither with convention nor heterodoxy. She hid herself away under her love for Mary and her ' father,' as she at that time believed Godwin to be. Her whole vitality was devoted to keeping the peace, for the constant friction was to her not so much a nervous as a moral and social distress.

W E now have the stage prepared for the fateful meeting
between Shelley and Mary Godwin, sometime in May 1814.
He was then twenty-two and she seventeen—mere children
by our present-day reckoning. In fact they were far from
children. Shelley at this time was world-weary, ill, and dis-
illusioned; suffering, as he confided to his friend Hogg, from
' the poet's premature old age.' He had crowded much into
his short life; not only a vast amount of emotional scholarship, but also the maturing of it into principles and practice.
He had imbibed knowledge, thought about it, and digested it,
and had already shown his quality by acting on his resolutions
and dragging his world about his ears. Only a great man, a
man possessing some abnormal strength and coherence of
conviction, could have done that. And since he was still
merely a boy in years, the only explanation of his power is to
confess our inability by saying he was inspired by genius.
It is a phrase coined by faith and intuition rather than intelligence, for logically it tells us nothing. It smacks of mystery-
mongering, and yet we know that it is honest and the only
symbol by means of which we can recognize that rare power.
Here is not the place to give his past history in detail. It is
sufficient to remember that he and Hogg had been expelled
from Oxford in March 1811 for refusing to repudiate their
authorship of the tract *The Necessity of Atheism*. Thence the
two boys had come to London and taken obscure lodgings off
Oxford Street in rooms that appealed to Shelley because one
of them had a wall-paper of trellised vines. He seems to

have had the inartistic taste typical in men of creative vigour.

The young men, after a short while together, were separated by their indignant parents, and Shelley was given an allowance of £200 a year and leave to go to the devil in his own way. His father was a singular character to have been the parent of such an original-minded young rebel. Timothy Shelley was peevish, vacillating yet obstinate, affectionate and tyrannical. He was class-bound and pedantic—both a social and a literary snob. His son, therefore, was a complete enigma to him; he appreciated neither his conduct, ideals, nor poetry. It was all subversive rubbish to him—and yet he loved the boy in his own way. He was what might be called an ' Egad, Sir ' type of country gentleman, the rather effete son of the vigorous, rapacious old reprobate Sir Bysshe, who had built up a huge fortune by two commercial marriages and obtained a baronetcy by serving the Whig interests of the blackguardly Duke of Norfolk.

At the time of these eventful days in Shelley's life, his old grandfather had left his seat, Castle Goring, standing empty, and was living in a small house near the Town Hall in Horsham, attended by one servant. He was a miser who sat with his money bags by him, only venturing out to a local tavern to overhear the evening's gossip. When he died, in 1815, £13,000 in notes were discovered between the leaves of books and sewn into the lining of his dressing-gown. It was natural that such a character should have no sympathy with a young man whose avowed object was to destroy the entail of the family estates, and to scatter his patrimony in largesse to needy philosophers; to aid the emancipation of Catholics in Ireland; to build breakwaters for sea-threatened Welsh villages. Yet such was the old man's perversity that he half-sympathized with his grandson for kicking over the traces, and poor Timothy in his dilemma accordingly got very little help from the head of the family.

Shelley had not been many months in London before he

disgraced himself still further by marrying the daughter of a coffee-house keeper. It is true the man had made a considerable fortune, for the coffee-house was a famous one, *The Mount*, by Grosvenor Square; but that would not make any difference to Timothy, so ' true-blue ' was he. The story of Shelley's entanglement is an intricate one, and involves the thorny problem of the character of his first wife. The question whether or not she was faithless to him is still an open one, with the evidence on Harriet's side, and happily it is not our concern here to try to answer it. Shelley believed that she was unfaithful; but the important point to note is that to Shelley the faithlessness of his wife brought no social or moral disgust, and that it awoke no jealousy. He regarded it as an absolute avowal that her love for him was dead, and he believed that to retain a relationship which had no spiritual reality was an act of cowardice, a mere truckling to habitual convention.

Harriet Westbrook had been a school-fellow of his two sisters at a seminary on Clapham Common. Apparently she was a vision that would break the heart of the most stolid youth. She never broke Shelley's, however, for he, being a poet, was made of sterner stuff. But her beauty staggered him, kindled in him that ecstasy of mind which gave his powerful intellect such apt lyrical expression. She was even the acknowledged beauty of the school, and was accordingly conscious of her charms. Shelley's sister says of her that she had a complexion ' quite unknown in those days, brilliant pink and white, and hair quite like a poet's dream, and Bysshe's peculiar admiration.' She was very endearing, too, with the disarming gestures and manners which are so often found in people who are fundamentally chilly and unmoved. And also, in common with that kind, she had a quick sympathy and a sharp intelligence, both, however, too shallow-rooted to survive a lack of appreciation. It is not sufficient to think of her as a doll; for she was a clever and beautiful woman; but she lacked real courage and confidence. There

was no spiritual resilience about her, and after the metabolic
reaction following the birth of her first child, she could no
longer make an effort to disguise her lack of faith in life.   In
consequence, at the most critical time of Shelley's monetary
troubles, she demanded the commonplace comforts of a
material world, and relinquished all attempts at mental discipline.   We can appreciate her misery at being forced to
recognize her defeat before the reproach-by-presence of
her husband.   This, and her bewildered love, must have
made her hate him.   But what she hated was the reflection of
herself which emanated from his fierce ardour and enthusiasm,
the merciless enemy of her inherent dolour and despair.

At the time of their meeting Shelley was unoccupied.   He
had, at the moment, no lost cause which he was espousing.
The reverberations of the triumphant disgrace at Oxford
were dying away.   It was a period for digesting his experi-
ences and reorganizing his ideas.   At such a time the intensity
of this operation made him demand sympathy and company.
Harriet found him in a quiescent mood, and she loved him
in that mood; he was mysterious, deep, unusual.   And then
there was Harriet's sister Eliza, who struck while the iron
was hot, and precipitated this ill-fated union.   ·

Eliza Westbrook was a strong-minded young woman,
ambitious and devoted to her family.   She had no illusions.
That is to say, she had a false idea of everything between
heaven and hell.   She really believed that Shelley was a
' bad ' man; but his vices were outweighed by his social
standing, and his prospective riches and title.   Her policy
with his ' fads ' was simply to over-ride them with common
sense and obstinate complacency.   She thought Shelley was
just weak-charactered and weak-minded—people of her
kind always do—and she hoped to break him in to suit the
social requirements of her sister, whom she deeply loved.
Had there been a way for Shelley and his wife to disguise
their incompatibility, it was barred by Eliza's counsel from
another world.

Harriet, perhaps moved by unconscious fear of the step she had taken in marrying Shelley, clung to her like a child, referring every difficulty, every quarrel, to her assured but foreign judgment. Shelley at first looked upon her as a soul to be reclaimed to the glorious principles of freedom, and he tolerated her worldly wisdom. But as he saw its effect upon Harriet be began to look upon this third party to the marriage as a spirit of evil, member of that blind, cruel, and stupid world which conducted the moral, political, and religious life of humanity with such tragic results. As the end of that unhappy tangle drew near, his mind became obsessed with hatred. She was used by him as a symbol of darkness just as Harriett's beauty had previously been used as a symbol of light.

In the spring of 1814 the domestic troubles of Shelley and Harriet were at their worst. She had by then given up all pretence at following his intellectual pilgrimage, and went her own way, seeking new and easier friendships. He had received a shock the previous summer, when she had refused to suckle her child. This morbid symptom in Harriett was followed by extravagant claims to be set up with a carriage, silver plate, and other paraphernalia appropriate to the wife of the prospective baronet. As despair and bafflement, and sense of failure, swept over her, she sank into a petulant idleness, neglecting the home and finding every pretext for picking quarrels. In the midst of this, however, Shelley, on learning that their Scottish marriage was likely to prove invalid, took steps to strengthen their union by re-marriage. In this he was helped by Godwin, now his friend as well as guide. The ceremony took place at St George's, Hanover Square, on the 24th March.

After this, they drifted apart, Harriet prompted by some demon of negation, Shelley in nervous reaction from the mere misery of the home. She seemed purposely to torture herself, for it is obvious that she loved Shelley. Perhaps acting on the vulgar advice of her sister, who had the prescription from some melodrama, she intended to regain Shelley's affection

by a show of coy coldness. With this intent she departed
to Bath with her father in July. Shelley still made appeals
to her affection, and was doing all in his power to prove that
they were parted only by a misunderstanding. But at that
time he met Mary Godwin, and all was changed.

F O R a long time past Mary Godwin had been forming a lofty preconception of Shelley. To be praised by her father was distinction indeed, and he had not hesitated to tell his daughter how remarkable were the mental powers of this young aristocrat, who had come into his impecunious life with generous offers of help. As early as 1812, Godwin had written to Shelley, saying: 'You cannot imagine how much all the females of my family—Mrs Godwin and three daughters—are interested in your letters and your history.' Shelley had since become the benefactor of the family, mortgaging his prospects by accepting the most ruinous post-obits in order to give Godwin ready money. All through the spring and early summer of 1814 he had been trying, by these means, to raise £3000 which was to stave off Godwin's bankruptcy.

Mary returned from Scotland in May, and she and Shelley met for the second time. The effect on both was instant. Shelley believed at this time that Harriet had given herself to another man—a soldier named Major Ryan. He felt, therefore, no obligation or moral tie. Had he done so, it is difficult to know how he would have fought it, for the intensity of his passion amounted almost to insanity. We must remember that he was never sane in the worldly sense of the word; that is to say, he was never cautious. Had he not been endowed with an abnormal intellectual power, his emotional nature would certainly have landed him in a madhouse.

For a time Godwin and his wife suspected nothing of the volcano that was rumbling beneath them. By July, however, the two lovers had come to an understanding. Mary saw the poet as a sick, tragic, and betrayed man. She also saw him, on occasion, shake off his weakness to take part in debates with the intellectual giants of the day and to hold his own with them, and throw new light on the subjects by brilliant flashes of poetic imagery and intuition. And with this she saw the almost eccentric kindness, the gentle manners, and genius for friendship which were so pronounced in him.

They confessed their tragic love for each other over her mother's grave in St Pancras Churchyard, where she was accustomed to go to spend her most sacred moments of solitude and to escape from home-life. Mary Wollstonecraft was a deity to both the young idealists, and gave their attraction a triple strength. Mary used to take her favourite books and read, as it were, under her mother's supervision.

Shelley followed her one day, and what was said between them no third person dare try to imagine.

He also gave her a copy of *Queen Mab*, writing in it: 'You see, Mary, I have not forgotten you,' and adding under the dedication to Harriet the words: 'Count Sloberdorf was about to marry a woman who, attracted solely by his fortune, proved *his* selfishness by deserting him in prison.' The mordant touch revealed in the word which I have italicised shows how bitterly his wife had wounded him.

Mary added, on the fly-leaf at the end of the volume:

'July 1814. This book is sacred to me, and as no other creature shall ever look into it, I may write in it what I please—yet what shall I write?—that I love the author beyond all the powers of expression, and that I am parted from him, dearest and only love—by that love we have promised to each other, although I may not be yours, I can never be another's. But I am thine, exclusively thine.

By the kiss of love, the glance none saw beside,
The smile none else might understand,
The whispered thought of hearts allied,
The pressure of the thrilling hand.

I have pledged myself to thee, and sacred is the gift. I
remember your words: You are now, Mary, going to mix
with many, and for a moment I shall depart, but in the
solitude of your chamber I shall be with you. Yes, you are
ever with me, sacred vision.

> But ah ! I feel in this was given
> A blessing never meant for me,
> Thou art too like a dream from·heaven
> For earthly love to merit thee ! '

It was unfortunate that Shelley's old friend Hogg should
have been the first to know of the great change which had
come about; for Hogg was a very susceptible man; he had
loved Harriet and told her so, and been forgiven. His
feelings must have been very confused as he recorded his
first acquaintance with Mary. He met Shelley in Cheapside,
and they walked together to Godwin's shop in Skinner
Street. Godwin was out and while they were waiting for
him in the bookroom, ' the door was partially and softly
opened. A thrilling voice called " Shelley ! " A thrilling
voice answered " Mary ! " And he darted out of the room,
like an arrow from the bow of the far-shooting king. A
very young female, fair and fair-haired, pale indeed, with a
piercing look, wearing a frock of tartan, an unusual dress in
London at the time, had called him out of the room. He was
absent a very short time—a minute or two, and then returned.
" Godwin is out, there is no use in waiting." So we continued our walk along Holborn. " Who was that, pray? "
I asked; " a daughter? " " Yes ! " " A daughter of William
Godwin? " " The daughter of Godwin and Mary." '

By July 14th Harriet was in town, full of foreboding at
having had no letters. When she met her husband he ex-
plained his position. Peacock says: ' The separation did not
take place by mutual consent. I cannot think that Shelley
ever so represented it. He never did so to me; and the
account which Harriett herself gave me of the entire proceed-

ing was definitely contradictory to any such supposition.
He might well have said, after seeing Mary Wollstonecraft
Godwin, " Ut vidi! ut perii! " Nothing that I ever read
in tale or history could ever present a more striking image of
a sudden, violent, uncontrollable passion, than that under
which I found him labouring when, at his request, I went up
from the country to call on him in London. Between his
old feelings for Harriet, *from whom he was not then separated*,
and his new passion for Mary, he showed in his looks, in his
gestures, in his speech, the state of a mind, suffering " like
a little kingdom, the nature of an insurrection! " His eyes
were bloodshot, and dress disordered. He caught up a bottle
of laudanum and said, " I never part from this! " He added,
" I am always repeating your lines from Sophocles—

> Man's happiest lot is not to be ;
> And when we tread life's thorny steep
> Most blest are they, who earliest free
> Descend to earth's eternal sleep."

Again he said, more calmly: " Everyone who knows me
must know that the partner of my life should be one who can
feel poetry and understand philosophy. Harriet is a noble
animal, but she can do neither." I said: " It always
appeared to me that you were very fond of Harriet." Without affirming or denying this, he answered: " But you did
not know how I hated her sister." '

c

5

AN ELOPEMENT OF THREE

ON July 28th 1814, a heavy brooding summer day, Mary and Claire left Skinner Street at five in the morning. Shelley was waiting for them at the corner of Hatton Garden with a post-chaise. Claire came to see Mary off, but she was persuaded to go with them, because she could speak French. Whether this addition to the party was proposed by Mary in a moment of fear, or by Shelley out of sheer benevolent excitement, is not known. It was one of those minor events which afterwards grow large and ominous. It was to rob Mary and Shelley of half the zest and joy of their short married life.

The journey to Dover was frequently interrupted because Mary was overcome by the heat, which worked on her disturbed nerves. They reached Dover at four in the afternoon, and Mary was revived by a dip in the sea. Finding that the packet would not sail until next day, they chartered a small fishing vessel and set out the same evening. Shelley was triumphant. To feel himself on the water was always an inspiration—like returning to like—and in addition he felt that in one bold move he had emancipated two human beings from a mode of life which oppressed them: and one of those two was the girl in whom he found a reconciliation between his passion and his ideals.

As they glided through the calm evening waters he must have felt that he was appreciably nearer the active and perfect manhood toward which he had always tortured himself. It is certain that from the moment of his union with Mary a remarkable development was shown in his character. Harriet, with all her beauty, charm, and affection, had helped him only negatively, by exactions on his patience and by forcing him into contact with inert actuality. During his life with her he had not shaken off the verbose and doctrinaire priggishness which is so frequently the chrysalis of genius. He was still a boy in years.

Mary was equipped, however, to be his intellectual lieutenant. Doubly gifted by heredity, she had been trained almost to breaking-point all her life. In every way she was able to satisfy Shelley's demand that his life-companion must be ' one who can feel poetry and understand philosophy.' A study of his letters shows the almost instantaneous change in him. The country of his brain cleared, and its vast riches lay spread out beneath the sun of his genius.

We left the lovers and their mischievous companion gliding happily across the Channel. By night, however, a wind arose, with heavy thunder squalls. Mary was ill again, and lay supine between Shelley's knees, while he revelled like a young Satan in the flashes of the lightning-swords as they broke on the thick water. The boat almost overturned, but towards dawn the storm fell, and the voyagers made into Calais. The first bout with his beloved adversary—that nature-image of himself—was a victory for Shelley.

Mrs Godwin followed them next day by the packet-boat. They heard from the hotel porter that a ' fat lady ' had arrived, ' who said he had run away with her daughter.' She spent the night with Claire, trying to persuade her to return. But Claire had tasted freedom—at some one else's expense—and she anticipated much more. So her mother went back alone, unhappily for the Shelleys.

The trio then proceeded to Paris, where they rested for a week. There Shelley sold his watch and chain; for with his characteristic insanity in relation to mundane affairs, he had left London with no money. An English ' milord ' in those days, however, seemed to be able to rake up ready cash wherever he might be dropped. Shelley borrowed some from a French business man, and was thus able to buy a donkey to carry their travelling bag. With this slender equipment the three set out to walk to Switzerland. The girls wore the only dresses they had, which were of black silk. The donkey, who was intended to carry Mary and the bag alternately, proved to be a sorry wreck and they had to sell him and buy a mule.

The black-silk party proceeded rapturously, living entirely in the moment; stopping as the mood took them, either to read from the one or two books which they had brought, or to picnic before some beautiful scene. All went well until one morning Shelley sprained his foot and had to ride the mule while the girls trudged along beside him all day, until they reached Troyes. While they rested there, Shelley wrote to Harriet : ' I write to urge you to come to Switzerland, where you will at least find one firm and constant friend, to whom your interests will be always dear—by whom your feelings will never be wilfully injured.' He also gave a description of the scenery through which they had passed, and mentioned the ravages left by Napoleon's thwarted ambitions. He then expressed the hope that he would be able to welcome her ' to some sweet retreat I will procure for you among the mountains.'

The travellers were still to be cheated, for having bought a *voiture* at Troyes, and hired a man to drive it, the latter treated them like truant children—they could have looked little else—and drove as he willed, careless whether his passengers were in the carriage or left behind. On one occasion he made them set out from a wretched inn at 3 a.m. Lack of money forced them to seek the cheapest shelter and food, and altogether they roughed it to the full.

At last they reached Switzerland, where, thanks to the good offices of Peacock at home, Shelley collected some more money. Peacock, however, was austere in his help at this time, for he liked Harriet and was piqued with Shelley for having left her at so difficult a time; for she was with child.

In Switzerland they idled for a while, dabbling with a little writing on a romantic tale, boating on the lakes, and climbing the mountain slopes. On August 25th they came to a village called Brunnen, and falling in love with its beauty, Shelley took a house for six months. The next day they suddenly decided to return to England, but had to wait another day as their linen was with the washerwoman. They thought it would be enchanting to return via the Rhine, with the consequence that they reached Rotterdam on 8th September ' horribly cheated ' and with only enough money to bargain for a sea passage home. Shelley spent the whole journey across in dispute with a fellow-passenger about the slave-traffic.

They reached Gravesend on the 14th without a penny. They had to take the boatman into their coach, and drive round London looking for money to pay him. Shelley found that during his absence Harriet had made havoc with his account at the bank, where he had left orders for her to draw what she wanted. Finally, the coach-load had to call on her, and Shelley reclaimed sufficient to free them from their difficulties. They then found lodgings in a street off Cavendish Square, bought a copy of Wordsworth's *Excursion* and spent the evening reading it, noting in their diary : ' Much disappointed. He is a slave.'

T H E story of the next nine months is one of suspense, trial, pain, and the triumph of faith. Shelley found that Godwin was not willing to forgive the injury dealt to his vanity, both as a father and a philosopher. Here was a man for the world to laugh at; an economist and moralist who could not order his own household. There was also an uglier rumour afloat, that he had sold his daughter Mary and Claire Clairmont to Shelley for £800 and £700 respectively. Claire's was a character on which rumour could feed with avidity, for it lacked the smallest element of discretion. Mrs Godwin was naturally furious—and this qualification can be used with a double meaning. Mary's sister Fanny was deeply wounded, both by the loss of her nearest and dearest, and by the fact that Mary had never confided in her.

All these complications closed the doors of Godwin's house to the young pair. The injured father consented to take Shelley's money only from a distance. It is a curious spectacle to see the philosopher of over sixty years of age proudly refusing to receive the young poet of twenty-two, yet at the same time eagerly allowing the lad to be compounded with usurers on his behalf. Debt was surely poisoning Godwin's character. At the moment debt was surely tarnishing the golden happiness of Shelley and Mary. Promissory notes, accepted for other people, came home to roost. Meanwhile Harriet was running up bills at shops and having the accounts sent to Shelley, while Claire was still sponging on him in their lodgings. In addition, the brother Charles

would frequently drop in for a small loan, and his example
was followed by a number of ' friends ' who realized that if
you would only provide Shelley with good intellectual
stimulus and argument, he would move the world to raise
a loan for you. Again and again Shelley had to disappear
into some obscure lodging off Snow Hill while the bailiffs
were out after him. On these occasions he could meet Mary
only furtively, by night, at street corners, or outside some
coffee house or inside St Paul's. Mrs Godwin added to their
comfort by paying obtrusive visits of curiosity to their lodging
windows, cruising up and down like an enemy squadron,
and then disappearing. Fanny, too, who had broken the
embargo laid by Godwin, alarmed them with a rumour
that Harriet was plotting to have Shelley arrested and Godwin ruined.

At this time, Mary was beginning to be weary and heavy
with child. Frequent bouts of weakness prevented her from
sharing as usual in Shelley's walks and studies. Limelight-
loving Claire monopolised him more and more, accompanying
him out of doors and keeping him up half the night talking
and arguing. She was quick-witted, and gifted with a wild
irresponsible humour that gave her a false appearance of
detachment. She could eat your bread, and you felt indebted
to her. She certainly kept up Shelley's harassed spirits,
for he liked her and her whimsical ways, while her hypnotic
hysteria appealed to his love of the fantastic—the ragged
edges of his huge imagination. Here is an incident recorded
in their diary by Shelley himself, which gives us a picture of
their bizarre life. It is like a scene from a Dostoevski novel:

' Friday, October 7 (Shelley's entry). Mary goes to bed
at half-past eight; Shelley sits up with Jane. At one o'clock
Shelley observes that it is the witching time of night; he
inquires soon after if it is not horrible to feel the silence of
night tingling in our ears; in half an hour the question is
repeated in a different form; at two they retire awestruck
and hardly daring to breathe. Shelley says to Jane, " Good

night "; his hand is leaning on the table; he is conscious
of an expression in his countenance which he cannot repress.
Jane hesitates.   " Good night " again.   She still hesitates.
" Did you ever read the tragedy of *Orra ?* " said Shelley.
" Yes.   How horribly you look!—turn your eyes off."
" Good night " again, and Jane runs to her room.   Shelley
unable to sleep kissed Mary, and prepared to sit beside her
and read till morning, when rapid footsteps descended the
stairs.   Jane was there; her countenance was distorted most
unnaturally by horrible dismay—it beamed with a whiteness that seemed almost like light; her lips and cheeks were of
one deadly hue; the skin of her face and forehead was drawn
into innumerable wrinkles—the lineaments of terror which
could not be contained; her hair came prominent and erect;
her eyes were wide and staring, drawn almost from the
sockets by the convulsion of the muscles; the eyelids were
forced in, and the eyeballs, without any relief, seemed as if
they had been newly inserted, in ghastly sport, in the sockets
of a lifeless head.   This frightful spectacle endured but for
a few moments—it was displaced by terror and confusion,
violent indeed, and full of dismay, but human.   She asked me
if I had touched her pillow (her tone was that of dreadful
alarm).   I said " No, no! if you will come into the room
I will tell you."   I informed her of Mary's pregnancy; this
seemed to check her violence.   She told me that a pillow
placed upon her bed had been removed, in the moment
that she turned her eyes away to a chair at some distance, and
evidently by no human power.   She was positive as to the
facts of her self-possession and calmness.   Her manner convinced me that she was not deceived.   We continued to sit
by the fire, at intervals engaging in awful conversation
relative to the nature of these mysteries.   I read part of
Alexy ; I repeated one of my own poems.   Our conversation,
although intentionally directed to other topics, irresistibly
recurred to these.   Our candles burned low; we feared they
would not last until daylight.   Just as the dawn was struggling

with moonlight, Jane remarked in me that unutterable expression which had affected her with so much horror before; she described it as expressing a mixture of deep sadness and conscious power over her. I covered my face with my hands, and spoke to her in the most studied gentleness. It was ineffectual; her horror and agony increased even to the most dreadful convulsions. She shrieked and writhed on the floor. I ran to Mary; I communicated in a few words the state of Jane. I brought her to Mary. The convulsions gradually ceased, and she slept. At daybreak we examined her apartment and found her pillow on the chair.'

At this time the inherent fineness and strength of Mary's character fully showed itself. She was not yet eighteen, with an illegitimate child in her womb. She was passionately in love with Shelley, yet overwhelmed with a sense of inferiority. She saw her greedy quasi-relative feeding on Shelley's brain and vitality, robbing her of his attentions, and of the precious solitude with him which was her right. In addition to this the hopelessly tangled mechanics of their mundane life must have increased her anxiety. On several occasions, for instance, the landlady had refused to send up any more meals until her account should be settled: and when, during one such incident Shelley had gone out to borrow money, he returned with—cake! Yet amid all this provocation she kept her serenity of heart and showed no tinge of jealousy. The studies which Shelley had induced her to take up, she still pursued—and that for her own sake. She was struggling bravely with Greek, Latin, and Italian, no small task when there were baby clothes to be thought about, and the close feather-touch within her of feverish hopes and forebodings. Here is her journal for November 1st :

' Learn Greek all morning. Shelley goes to the 'change. People want their money; won't send up dinner, and we are all very hungry. Jane goes to Hookham. Shelley and I talk about her character. Jane returns without money.

Goes to Peacock, to send him to us with some eatables; he is out. Charles promises to see her. She returns to Pancras; he goes there, and tells the dismal state of the Skinner Street affairs. Shelley goes to Peacock's; comes home with cakes. Wait till Hookham sends money to pay the bill. Shelley returns to Pancras. Have tea and go to bed. Shelley goes to Peacock's to sleep.'

Occasionally they snatched a morning, or even a whole day together, sipping each moment of it with eagerness. Such an oasis in the desert was Sunday, November 6th, recorded in the diary:

' Talk to Shelley. He writes a great heap of letters. Read part of *St. Leon*. Talk with all the evening; this is a day devoted to Love in idleness. Go to sleep early in the evening. Shelley goes away a little before 10.'

A month later, however, Mary suffers a severe test of her equanimity and cannot suppress an exclamation of bitterness:

' December 6th. Very unwell. Shelley and Claire walk out as usual, to heaps of places. Read *Agathon*, which I do not like as well as *Peregrine*. A letter from Hooker, to say that Harriet has been brought to bed of a son and heir. Shelley writes a number of circular letters of this event, which ought to be ushered in with ringing of bells, etc., for it is the son of his *wife*. Hogg comes in the evening, I like him better though he vexes me by his attachment to sporting. A letter from Harriet confirming the news, in a letter from a *deserted wife ! !* and telling us he has been born a week.'

Brooding over the contrast which would be afforded between this child and her own unborn, she sank into despondency. It was a mood common with her; for while she was brave, energetic, and persistent, there was a certain lowness and debility in her constitution which made her a dependent rather than an assertive personality. She dreaded loneliness, and without encouragement was prone to work on mechanically in despair and bereft of enthusiasm. It was this pathetic shortcoming which made her, in later years, somewhat querulous and inclined to irritate her more robust friends. There are signs that even Shelley, with all his devotion to her, felt these moods of hers as a burden, and his reaction from them often resulted in callous gestures of revolt.

Sir Bysshe Shelley died on January 5th 1815. Shelley, accompanied by Claire, immediately went down to his father's home at Field Place, and was refused admittance. Instead of leaving indignantly, he seated himself on the doorstep and drawing Mary's copy of Milton from his pocket, began to read *Comus*, and was only to be moved by the persuasion of the family doctor. After two months of coming and going between lawyers' offices, it was finally agreed that Shelley should receive a sum of £7400, and an annuity during his father's lifetime of £1000 a year. Picturesque poverty, therefore, came to an end, and Shelley was able to stave off the harpies who had been waiting so long and so patiently. He also settled £200 a year on Harriett.

The last few months of strain and excitement had told sadly on Mary's health, and on February 22nd a seven-month's child was born. On the day of its birth the little infant took its place in the intellectual life of that almost disembodied household, for friends and members of the menage still mingled indiscriminately in the long symposium of mental delights which was to end only with the final departure of Shelley, its life-spirit. He records for that day: ' Maie perfectly well and at ease. The child is not quite seven months; the child is not expected to live. Shelley sits up with Maie, much exhausted and agitated. Hogg sleeps here.'

For some unaccounted reason, the Shelleys changed their lodgings on March 2nd, *a week after the confinement !* Here are the entries for the following three days. Could anything paint more vividly the youth, inexperience, and complete lack of any love of comfort, which these ardent people possessed ?

'*March 4th.* Read, talk, and nurse. Shelley reads the life of Chaucer. Hogg comes in the evening and sleeps.

March 5th. Shelley and Claire go to town. Hogg here all day. Read *Corinne* and nurse my baby. In the evening talk. Shelley finishes the life of Chaucer. Hogg goes at 11.

March 6th. Find my baby dead. Send for Hogg. Talk. A miserable day. In the evening read *The Fall of the Jesuits.* Hogg sleeps here.'

Mary had been trained to an abnormal asceticism, and Reason had been held up to her as the most *real* thing in life. Her union with Shelley had only intensified this discipline. How severely she must have schooled herself against grief is shown by the struggle she made to force herself down to her studies, and to prevent sad dreams, by day and by night, from sapping her will. She did not always succeed, for she writes on March 19th: 'Dream that my little baby came to life again; that it had only been cold, and that we rubbed it before the fire, and it lived. Awake and find no baby. I think about the little thing all day.'

All this time they had been trying to get rid of Claire, who with her erratic egotism and her violent moods had become unbearable. Shelley and Mary were in despair, when suddenly, in May, Claire decided to go off alone and live the rustic life in a Devonshire cottage. There she remained in a sort of humorously tragic retirement, writing delightful letters—at which art she excelled—and scandalising local propriety by her unconventional habits. In the spring of 1816 she returned to London and sought out Lord Byron, thinking with his help to get on the stage. She failed in her purpose, as also in persuading him that she wanted his advice about writing a novel. Finally she threw off all pretence, and suggested that they should spend a night together, 'although she did not expect him to love her.' Byron's sultry interest was sufficiently roused for him to indulge in a short liaison with her, with the result that she returned to the Shelley's in even more menacing a condition than before.

Mary records her exit with a very eloquent phrase: ' I begin a new journal with our regeneration.' For the next twelve months she was to have real calm and happiness, the only period of her life that was comparatively free from calamitous accidents and reverses.

7

I N June they left London for Torquay, and for a month they lived absolutely together, with and for each other. Their troubles had added intimacy to their passion—that spiritual and smooth-motioned intimacy which is the most perfect gesture of marriage. For once they were able to let ' sweet Fancy roam ' without a sense of danger.

The result of this fruitful and careless indolence was that Shelley's suppressed nervous power surged up with an added strength and maturity, and he entered on a new stage of self-development. He planned *Alastor*, or *The Spirit of Solitude*. It is a spacious poem, and is one of the first to show that intense intellectual speed breasted by emotional rhythm, which are the dominant forces in his work. In this poem, he breaks asunder the two parts of his universe, Poetry and Philosophy, and introduces the third element of Love. So he vindicates his own growth, and gives his magnificent mental and spiritual machine a more definite direction. As he says in his preface : ' His mind is at length suddenly awakened and thirsts for intercourse with an intelligence similar to itself. He imagines to himself the Being whom he loves.' This record of change, however, embracing

> ' Nature's vast frame, the web of human things,
> Birth and the grave that are not as they were '

was not actually started until they were settled in a house at Bishopsgate, near Windsor Forest, where they had Peacock for neighbour. Peacock lingered about the neighbourhood all his life and subsequently sheltered his daughter Mrs

Nicholls and her second husband George Meredith there—
nearly forty years later.

The hot summer was made the most of; and a boating
excursion was taken for ten days up to the source of the
Thames. Shelley, impetuous as ever, wanted to go on, by
canal and any helpful stream, until they reached the Clyde!
Charles Clairmont, who was one of the party, records that
they spent a day at Oxford, visiting the Bodleian Library,
and the Clarendon Press, and the rooms ' where the two noted
infidels, Shelley and Hogg (now happily excluded from the
society of the present residents) pored, with the incessant and
unwearied application of the alchymist, over the certified
and natural boundaries of human knowledge.' He added:
' We have all felt the good effects of this jaunt, but in Shelley
the change is quite remarkable; he has now the ruddy,
healthy complexion of the autumn upon his countenance,
and he is twice as fat as he used to be.' Shelley produced a
good poem, *A Summer Evening*, written at Lechlade.

All this must have been paradise to Mary; for she was so
young that the physical roughing of the holiday would be no
hardship. She felt, indeed, that the calm wind of their
happiness had

> ' .   .   .   .   swept from the wide atmosphere
> Each vapour that obscured the sunset's ray.'

By the end of the year, however, clouds were gathering
again. Harriet and her family applied for the custody of the
two children. Shelley now distrusted her profoundly and
dreaded the prospect of his children being brought up in an
atmosphere of intellectual slovenliness, superstition, and sub-
mission to creature comfort. He refused his wife's request,
and the matter was taken to law. He thereupon sought his
father's help; but Sir Timothy, guided always by his careful
solicitor, refused to touch the affair. Indeed, his only interest
was to start further litigation over the family estate so that
his son should be prevented from burdening it with debts.

In addition to these gathering worries, Godwin was proving very intractable. He would not see his daughter and her lover, though during the year Shelley had to sell another annuity in order to raise money to help him. Since both Mary and Shelley were blind to his faults—blaming Mrs Godwin for them—this estrangement was very grievous and it crowned the distress they felt at the wholesale dropping away of friends. It must be remembered that malign rumour and gossip had fastened on them with eagerness, for to people the world with demons was a popular fancy at that time—a fashion reflected in the romantic and sentimental art of the age. The fact that Shelley had run away with two young girls was too much to be overlooked by the people who had already been aggravated by his theories.

This ostracism was felt keenly by Shelley and Mary, for they both were full of candour, optimism, and innocence; three cardinal qualities of the creative spirit. In addition, their sensitiveness was increased by the birth of a son, in January; for the coming of children tends to make us more sociable and gregarious. Early in the spring Claire returned to them, and finding them in the mood for a change of residence, persuaded them to take her to Geneva, where she knew Byron was also likely to be stopping. Shelley was not unwilling to meet Byron, for he admired the grandeur and speed of this regal mind.

Arrived in Geneva, they lodged in the Hotel Secheron, where they spent the days quietly. Mary writes, in a long letter afterwards printed with *The Journal of a Six Weeks' Tour*: ' We have hired a boat, and every evening at about six o'clock, we sail on the lake, which is delightful, whether we glide on a glassy surface or are speeded along by a strong wind. The waves of this lake never afflict me with that sickness that deprives me of all enjoyment in a sea voyage; on the contrary, the tossing of out boat raises my spirits and inspires me with unusual hilarity. Twilight here is of short duration, but we at present enjoy the benefit of an increasing moon, and seldom return until ten o'clock, when, as we approach the shore, we are saluted by the delightful scent of flowers and new-mown grass, and the chirp of the grass-hoppers, and the song of the evening birds.'

Soon after this letter was written, Byron, attended by his physician, an Italian named Polidori, arrived at Geneva. There Shelley first met him and revelled in the intellectual feast. He found someone worthy of his steel. Byron, however, brought the disadvantages of fame with him, and the Shelleys discovered themselves to be too much in the public eye to be comfortable. So they crossed the lake to a country cottage called Maison Chapuis, turning their backs on the shy Mont Blanc and facing the Jura Mountains.

They were soon followed by Byron, who had also grown weary of sightseers and lion-hunters. He took a house called the Villa Diodati, which stood on a hill above the Shelleys' cottage and was separated from it by a vineyard. That short holiday was one of the most invigorating periods in Shelley's life. Here were gathered together all the good things which he desired : an intimate relationship, born of pas-sionate understanding; a commerce with an intellect sharp and swift as his own, and certainly one that could lead him by reason of its greater objectivity and multiplicity of interest; a natural scenery on the grand scale; and the pre-sence of water. There were inspired traffickings to and fro, through the vineyard; argument, readings, urging, and sug-gestion. And also there were laughter and music, and boating on the lake, with daily expeditions and picnics.

Shelley seems to have been the only man to whom Byron was willing to play second fiddle. Shelley's superior self-education, an edifice constructed with the unerring power of his noble imagination, made Byron feel that in comparison his own equipment was that of a broad but shallow journalist. But in many ways Byron was the bigger man. He was more four-square, more various, more of an epitome of humanity, than was Shelley. He had not Shelley's concentrated and

D

highly spiritual force; but his instincts were bold and noble.
He trod, and made the heavens shake, though often he did
not know where he was stumbling.

Small wonder that Mary was contented to be a picker-up
of crumbs at the nightly sittings of the two poets. She seemed
also to be secretly afraid of Byron, appalled by his occasional
outbursts of violent egoism. She not infrequently absented
herself from the evening gatherings, feeling that Byron did
not want her there. This little touch of the persecution-
mania never left her, and later in life it added to the torments
of loneliness a very decided strain of morbidity. Perhaps
her early days, under the five-thumbed hands of good Mrs
Godwin, may have had something to do with this malaise.

In spite of these occasional feelings of 'odd-man-out,'
however, this holiday was the most happy and fruitful period
of Mary's life. In it she conceived the work which is her
most personal claim to immortality. It was the habit of the
friends to read tales of mystery and horror to each other during
the evenings spent at Diodati. They found themselves so
amused by these tales—a *genre* which had sprung out of the
Romantic attitude toward Nature and super-Nature—that
they proposed amongst themselves that each should produce
a story in this kind. Byron and Shelley both began, but their
enthusiasm waned—how could it do otherwise—and only
the physician Polidari persisted in the attempt. He produced
a tale that had a certain vogue owing to the popular misbelief
that Byron had written it. When the real author was discovered it died a quick death. Mary was not so facile at
beginning, for she failed to find a theme. Every morning
she was asked, banteringly, if she had begun, but she had,
sensitively, to confess her failure. During one of the con-
versations between Byron and Shelley, various philosophical
doctrines were discussed, amongst them, as Mary tells us,
'the nature of the principle of life,' and whether there was
any probability of its ever being discovered and communicated. They talked of the experiment of Dr Darwin, who

preserved a piece of vermicelli in a glass case until by some extraordinary means it began to move with voluntary motion. Not thus, after all, would life be given. Perhaps a corpse would be re-animated; galvanism had given token of such things; perhaps the component parts of a creature might be manufactured, brought together, and endued with vital warmth.

'Night waned upon this talk, and even the witching hour had gone by, before we returned to rest. When I placed my head upon the pillow I did not sleep, nor could I be said to think. My imagination, unbidden, possessed and guided me, gifting the successive images that arose in my mind with a vividness far beyond the usual bounds of reverie. I saw with shut eyes, but acute mental vision—I saw the pale student of unhallowed arts kneeling beside the thing he had put together—I saw the hideous phantasm of a man stretched out, and then, on the working of some powerful engine, show signs of life, and stir with an uneasy, half vital motion. Frightful must it be; for supremely frightful would be the effect of any human endeavour to mock the stupendous mechanism of the Creator of the world. His success would terrify the artist; he would rush away from his odious handiwork, horror-stricken. He would hope that, left to itself, the slight spark which he had communicated would fade; that this thing which had received such imperfect animation would subside into dead matter; and he might sleep in the belief that the silence of the grave would quench forever the transient existence of the hideous corpse which he had looked upon as the cradle of life. He sleeps; but he is awakened; he opens his eyes; behold the horrid thing stands at his bedside, opening his curtains, and looking on him with yellow, watery, but speculative eyes.

'I opened mine in terror. The idea so possessed my mind that a thrill of fear ran through me, and I wished to exchange the ghastly image of my fancy for the realities around. I see them still; the very room, the dark *parquet*, the closed shutters,

with the moonlight struggling through, and the sense I had
that the glassy lake and the white high Alps were beyond. I
could not so easily get rid of my hideous phantom; still it
haunted me. I must try to think of something else. I
recurred to my ghastly story—my tiresome unlucky ghost-
story. Oh! if I could only. contrive one which would
frighten my reader as I myself had been frightened that night!
'Swift as light and as cheering was the idea that broke
in upon me. " I have found it! What terrified me will
terrify others; and I need only describe the spectre which
had haunted my midnight pillow." On the morrow I
announced that I had *thought of a story*.' Such, in her
own words is the history of the genesis of her tale of *Frankenstein*.

Shortly after this Shelley and Byron went for a boating
trip round the lake. During this excursion Byron wrote the
Prisoner of Chillon and the third canto of *Childe Harold*,
while Shelley made his preparations for writing the *Hymn to
Intellectual Beauty*. During that fruitful journey, Mary
remained at Chapuis, and began to put her vision into shape.
In July, she accompanied her husband to Chamounix. From
that time until her romance was finished, she carried her
manuscript about with her, adding to it the half-assimilated
ideas which her young and avid mind picked up from day to
day. She must have enjoyed writing the book, for her avowed
intention to make the reader's flesh creep was highly successful.

Frankenstein, an adolescent's version of the eternal story
of Man's attempt to create human life, must be considered as
a permanent addition to the world's literature of the macabre.
It has in it a touch of the genius of Edgar Allen Poe, to which
is added a tender ideality and a heart-rending effort to escape
from the toils of her own tragic conception. She made the
book a battleground for her own unreconciled emotional
and intellectual struggles—a not uncommon process with
artists in the early stages of their development. One feels

that throughout the tale, she is consciously trying to rise above the atmosphere and the technique of determinism in which her childhood had been spent. This effort egged on her girlish romanticism to indulge in glaring improbabilities in the construction of her story. Shelley, with his paper-boat and fire-balloon fantasy ever unappeased, was not the critic to discourage this weakness, and in consequence the book is marred very seriously by a certain haste, an indolence, a vagueness of construction. For instance, Frankenstein, the ardent young chemist, who after only *two years* of study has achieved his purpose, is allowed to lose sight of his monstrous creature until nearly half-way through the book. He almost forgets the shock which had nearly bereft him of his reason when he discovered the living result of his tampering with God's universe. It was not until the monster, in a fit of blind, pitiable, and hopeless ferocity, had wrought havoc by murdering Frankenstein's brother and causing a beloved nurse to be executed for the deed, that the young creator realized the full responsibility of his action.

Apart, however, from the technique of the tale, which in spite of its faults is a good narrative, the interest of the book is that it brings into a clear focus certain qualities peculiar to its author. I have already hinted that Mary was inclined to be a ' wet-blanket ' both to herself and those around her, in spite of her periodic gaiety of heart and happy sociability. Frankenstein suddenly became the victim of his own endeavours. From the moment of his great achievement, he was persecuted by the creature of his genius. That creature was a symbol of Mary's overtrained intellectual conscience. The child of her mother, wilful, impetuous, and generous to all-comers, she had been taught by her father to distrust these intuitions and impulses. This teaching had received only too convincing a justification by experience; for life with the noisy, blunt-souled Clairmonts meant indifference towards, and satire of, her open-hearted nature. With all her passion, therefore, she could never quite trust the people she loved, and in consequence her relationship with them, in spite of her ample profferings and heroic devotion, always hid yet half-revealed a quality of strain, a final reserve. Dimly realizing this, she redoubled her efforts at intimacy and gave them a touch of fever which sometimes startled the people toward whom they were directed. She clung tenaciously, when in reality she was capable of standing alone, and the result was that where she loved most deeply, she sometimes a little repelled. This characteristic may serve to explain Shelley's mood of callousness toward her at the moment when she most needed his support. It may also help us to understand Byron's sudden impatience with her, Jane Williams' treachery, and Trelawny's occasional outbursts of antipathy so noticeable in their interruption of his deep lover-like sympathy.

Frankenstein, following his obsession by the shadow of his monster—a being, by the way, whom Mary never clearly articulates, so little is she master of it—says that 'a blight had come over my existence. Company was irksome to me; when alone, I could fill my mind with the sights of heaven and earth; the voice of my friend soothed me, and I could thus cheat myself into a transitory peace. But busy uninteresting joyous faces brought back despair to my heart. I saw an insurmountable barrier placed between me and my fellow-men.' This is a very decided symptom of nervous malady and it comes direct from the soul of Frankenstein's author; it is a confession that she was aware of, and ashamed of, her attacks of timidity and jealousy. A most striking example of this miserable delight in self-torture is shown by her anticipation of disaster. At the time that she was writing this book, the baby William was in the tenderest and most intimate stage of dependent infancy. The mite of five months of age was passionately tended—but not very knowledgeably or hygienically—by both his parents. It is almost inconceivable that Mary could allow herself to introduce a baby boy into her book; deliberately call him William, describe

him in terms identical with those in which she portrays her
own child in one of her letters—and then let Frankenstein's
monster waylay this innocent in a woodland dell and murder
him by strangling. She pictures the fictitious child thus:
' I wish you could see him; he is very tall of his age, with
sweet laughing blue eyes, dark eyelashes, and curling hair.
When he smiles, two little dimples appear on each cheek,
which are rosy with health.' Only a few months later she
writes to Shelley : ' The blue eyes of your sweet Boy are
staring at me while I write this; he is a dear child, and you
love him tenderly.'

Now let us see how she permits herself to indulge in the
horrible self-torture of lingering over the child's death—we
purposely confuse the real with the fictitious infant. Frankenstein, confronted by the monster, has to listen to its tale of
misery and dumb aspiration toward full manhood. Repelled
with terror and loathing by the few human beings whom it
approaches in a craving for help and pity, it turns against
the whole race of what it considers to be beautiful but unjust
humanity. In particular its hatred is concentrated on the
person who has given it such a hideous and mocking sem-
blance of life. So might an artificial rose, hammered from
some base metal, and enamelled with mineral colours, hate the
engineer who made it and threw it carelessly into a garden-
bed where the real buds breathed, dewy-hearted. The
wretched mechanism of parchment face and lustreless eye
describes its furtive travels:

' But my toils now draw near a close; and in two months
from this time I reached the environs of Geneva.

' It was evening when I arrived and I retired to a hiding-
place among the fields that surround it, to meditate in what
manner I should apply to you. I was oppressed by fatigue
and hunger, and far too unhappy to enjoy the gentle breezes
of evening, or the prospect of the sun setting behind the
stupendous mountains of Jura.

' At this time a slight sleep relieved me from the pain of

reflection, which was disturbed by the approach of a beautiful child, who came running into the recess I had chosen, with all the sportiveness of infancy. Suddenly, as I gazed on him, an idea seized me, that this little creature was unprejudiced, and had lived too short a time to have imbibed a horror of deformity. If, therefore, I could seize him, and educate him as my companion and friend, I should not be so desolate in this peopled earth. Urged by this impulse, I seized the boy as he passed and drew him towards me. As soon as he beheld my form, he placed his hands before his eyes and uttered a shrill scream; I drew his hand forcibly from his face, and said, " Child, what is the meaning of this? I do not intend to hurt you; listen to me."

' He struggled violently. "Let me go," he cried. " Monster! ugly wretch! you wish to eat me, and tear me to pieces—You are an ogre—Let me go, or I will tell my papa."

' " Boy, you will never see your father again; you must come with me."

' " Hideous monster! Let me go. My papa is a Syndic —he is M. Frankenstein—he will punish you. You dare not keep me."

' " Frankenstein! you belong then to my enemy—to him toward whom I swore eternal revenge; you shall be my first victim."

' The child still struggled and loaded me with epithets which carried despair to my heart; I grasped his throat to silence him and in a moment he lay dead at my feet.

' I gazed at my victim, and my heart swelled with exultation and hellish triumph.'

Apart from admiration for the dramatic tension which the author creates by previously enlisting our sympathies for the virtue-seeking monster, we can only be repelled by her entertaining such an idea and by her lingering over its exploitation, while her own child lay in its cradle by her side. There is a morbidity in the conception which makes us feel that

Mary must have had, latent in her nature, a touch of that
spiritual debility and inertia which had so put Shelley's first
wife, Harriet, out of love with life as to make her seek self-
destruction.   From this we are tempted to speculate what
quality Shelley possessed which could call out this similar
strain from two women of such opposite natures.   Did his
alarming detachment and impersonality, his unflickering
flame of enthusiasm, scorch and shrivel up the tendrils by
which both these somewhat parasitic women fixed themselves
into the tree of life?   And was Mary's picture of the miseries
and remorse of Frankenstein a reproach toward Shelley for
his inhuman devotion to the austere rites of poetry and
philosophy?

8

LOSS AND RELEASE

o n August 28th the Platonic banquet came to an end, and the party returned to England. The main object of the expedition, which was to induce Byron to make a settlement on Claire, had been unsuccessful, for the poet had turned with loathing from this self-interested young woman, with her erotic tantrums, and her acid wit which no doubt pricked his skin.

The return to England was a return to trials and responsibilities for Mary. It is so difficult to realize, when we remember her conduct during the troubled times which were now to befall her, that she was only a girl of nineteen years of age. She had already borne two children, survived the opprobrium of her illicit life with Shelley, held his dangerous and hovering love for two years, pursued her studies of philosophy and languages, and commenced a novel which has since become a classic.

The fatigues of the return journey revealed Claire's condition, and accordingly Mary took her with the baby William and his Swiss nurse Elise to Bath, while Shelley once more went house-hunting, with Peacock's house as his headquarters. The young couple were deeply embarrassed, for Claire's pregnancy was calculated to add plausibility to the malicious rumours which had caused the flight from Bishopsgate in the spring.

Affairs in the Godwin household now came to one of their periodical crises. Earlier in the year Shelley had promised

Godwin a sum of £300. He now found that he could raise
no more than £200, and Godwin was left to find the remainder of the bill which had become due. Mary's sister
Fanny had to bear the brunt of the domestic storms which
were precipitated by the strain. Mrs Godwin nagged and
Godwin sank deeper and deeper into his self-protective
gloom. Fanny could stand the strain no more, and made an
effort to run away to her aunts in Dublin. But they refused
to have her. This refusal seemed to close the door of reality
to her, and she escaped into a world of fantasy, giving
up all her efforts to keep the hearts of her beloved few,
Godwin, Mary, Shelley, and Claire, in harmony with each
other.

She left home suddenly one day in October, ostensibly to
go to her aunt in Ireland. She had previously written to
Mary a long letter, trying to excuse the conduct of Mrs
Godwin. Now, however, she wrote a note from Bristol,
which caused Shelley to go there post-haste. In it, she laid
bare the misery which had accumulated over her life, a
burden none had shared with her because none had been
aware of its presence, so deceptive had been her cheerful
altruism. Blow after blow had fallen; she had lost Mary,
her one earthly bond with her mother; and she had learned
that Godwin, to whom she had devoted her life, was not her
father. So came at last her resolution to ' depart immediately
to the spot from which I hope never to return.' These
words she wrote from Bristol. The next day she proceeded
to Swansea and took a bedroom at an inn. The following
morning she was found dead with a laudanum bottle beside
her.

Mary seems to have been the bravest of those affected by
the tragedy, for Shelley's health broke down under the
shock, while Claire, her confinement approaching, sank into
a torpid condition of gloom. Godwin, who had loved Fanny
as much as his own child, nevertheless was most occupied
in his mind to keep the news from spreading abroad. For a

philosopher, he was unduly sensitive to conventional opinion.
Mrs Godwin, of course, put the whole blame on Shelley,
who for her was a symbol of the Devil. She accused him of
having awakened Fanny's love, and consequent jealousy of
Mary.

Two months of gloom and depression followed, bravely
lived down by Mary, who applied herself to the composition
of *Frankenstein*. Shelley meanwhile resumed his house
hunting—a perpetual occupation for him during their eight
years together. Mary wrote to him encouragingly, offering
ideal suggestions; 'a house (with a lawn) near a river or
lake, noble trees, or divine mountains, a garden, and *absentia*
Claire.'

On 14th December Shelley returned to her at Bath, and
on the following day received the news that Harriet had
drowned herself in the Serpentine, thereby succumbing to
the drag of her fate which had lured her from girlhood to this
deed. As early as 1811, Shelley had written that his reason
for marrying her was a dread of this inertia at the bottom of
her mind. 'Suicide was with her a favourite theme.' The
landlady at the inn where she last stayed said that she was
with child, but the evidence at the inquest does not bear
out this statement. It seems probable, however, that she had
been living with a man, who had deserted her shortly before
her death. The poor child, victim of a slothful and sensual
temperament, gay, good-hearted, and beautiful, was only
twenty-one when she threw herself into the arms of death,
as the only power who would not force her to the hateful
effort of self-reliance. In spite of the determined champion-
ship by Shelley's male friends—particularly Hogg and
Peacock—one cannot help feeling that she had something
of the temperament of Rossetti's *Jenny*, the eternal plaything,
tragically kind, with that passionate affection which a child
can give, fierce as a fire of straw. And yet there is always
an enigma about her. She showed so much intelligence
in her letters—but again, that was the *brightness* of a child,

rather than the burden-sharing appreciation which a com-
passionate adult should give.

To Shelley she was a husk of the past.   He loved her only
with a small fraction of his being.   He had nothing to forgive
—but at the same time he had no remorse and no regrets.

MARY had known Harriet hardly at all, and her reaction to the tragedy could only be solicitude for her husband, partly mitigated by a half-suppressed feeling of relief. Shelley was now free to marry her, and so to close the breach which separated her from her father. Both Godwin and his wife attended the ceremony on 30th December. The married couple returned immediately to Bath, where Claire had been left waiting for her hour to come. On 13th January, she gave birth to Byron's child, Allegra, a lovely little creature who was to capture everybody's heart by her beauty and happy disposition. Shelley, with his large impersonal benevolence, took on the duties of a father to the infant, thus giving the gossips a final convincing argument in evidence of his depravity. These current rumours, added to his well-known 'atheistic' theories, were now responsible for a bitter grief. Immediately after Harriet's death, both Shelley and Mary set about to obtain custody of his children, Ianthe and Charles —the latter heir-presumptive to the estates. They naturally thought that their marriage would have propitiated public opinion; but it was not so. The Westbrooks fought hard, and the prejudice of the court was against the children's father. The result of the suit was that the infants were made wards in Chancery, and put under the care of a country parson. Shelley was allowed to see them only twelve times a year, in the presence of their guardians.

This harassing business occupied them until March 1817, and during that time the only relief they found from their

presagings of defeat was in the intellectual companionship of
Godwin's circle—*the* circle of that time. They now also
knew Leigh Hunt, and his happy-go-lucky wife Marianne,
to whom Mary became much attached. At the Hunts'
they met Keats, Lamb, and Hazlitt, none of whom liked
Shelley. Keats was class-conscious, touched with the horrible
virus of suspicion which one feels towards the university man
when oneself has been differently educated. There may,
too, have been the sense of self-preservation which marks
the strong, creative personality. Keats absorbed his philosophy
through his skin, by a diffused general consciousness in the
manner of Shakespeare. Shelley was like Dante, concentrated into a mathematical vigour. The two methods would
not mix.

Lamb, the charming bachelor, the unique English
eccentric, was offended by Shelley's shrill voice, which soared
and broke like that of a boy at the age of puberty. Hazlitt
was even less charitable, for he complained of Shelley's
haggard and sickly appearance, as though a body that housed
so super-human a spirit should be expected to show no sign
of strain.

After Shelley's death, however, he made up for this
antagonism by a tribute which appeared in the *Edinburgh
Review*, where he wrote: ' Mr Shelley was a remarkable
man. His person was a type and shadow of his genius. His
complexion fair, golden, freckled, seemed transparent with
an inward light, and his spirit within him

" so divinely wrought
That you might almost say his body thought."

He reminded those who saw him of some of Ovid's fables.
His form, graceful and slender, drooped like a flower in the
breeze. But he was crushed beneath the weight of thought
which he aspired to bear, and was withered in the lightning-
glare of a ruthless philosophy!' Hazlitt could not prophesy

how he was to master that weight, and to tame the lightning-glare of Godwin's baleful fires.

Horace Smith, a wealthy stock-broker and amateur of letters, made Shelley's acquaintance at this time, and became a good friend to the poet and also to Mary.

As some recompense for their recent indignities, material circumstances became a little easier for the Shelleys, and they found their days agreeably occupied with visits (their marriage had been a compliment to many people), musical parties, and nights at the opera.

At last they found a house, which Shelley took on a twenty-years lease, and in the spring of 1817 they settled at Marlow. Thus began the last phase of their life in England. As the summer approached, their spirits grew calmer, and they were both able to work. Their house had a garden and an orchard, with yew trees and cypresses, and a noble cedar which can still be seen there. A riparian peace hovered over the neighbourhood—the very quality which always set Shelley to work. He now wrote his great poem *The Revolt of Islam*, or, as it was first called, ' Laon and Cythna.' The dedication, consisting of fourteen Spenserian stanzas, contains a portrait of Mary which seems to divine the very essence of her nature, shorn of all its weaknesses.

' And what art thou ? I know, but dare not speak,
     Time may interpret to his silent years.
Yet in the paleness of thy thoughtful cheek,
     And in the light thine ample forehead wears,
     And in thy sweetest smiles, and in thy tears,
     And in thy gentle speech, a prophecy
Is whispered, to subdue my fondest fears ;
     And thro' thine eyes, even in thy soul I see
A lamp of vestal fire burning internally.

They say that thou wert lovely from thy birth
     Of glorious parents, thou aspiring child :
     I wonder not—for One then left this earth
     Whose life was like a setting planet mild,

Which clothed thee in the radiance undefiled
Of its departing glory ; still her fame
Shines on thee through the tempest dark and wild
Which shakes these latter days ; and thou canst claim
The shelter, from thy Sire, of an immortal name.'

While Shelley was engaged on this long poem, Mary finished *Frankenstein*, and in May went to London to arrange for its publication. She did not neglect her reading, however, and every evening she would discuss her studies with her husband, who would pour his eloquent fire into them, and make her work glorious to her. The slightest sign of anyone being interested in the life of ideas inspired him immediately. All through this active-sleepy summer he needed such inspiration, for his faith and optimism were at their lowest ebb. The recent disasters and the constant worry of having to find money for Godwin—that prince of cadgers ; the strain of supporting Claire and her unfortunate child; all these things, combined with constant asceticism, broke his health, and he was threatened with lung trouble.

After finishing *Frankenstein*, Mary applied herself to the task of completing and preparing for publication her *Journal of a Six Weeks' Tour*, the record of their honeymoon. It appeared in December.

With all their writing and study, they found time to help their poorer neighbours—no small task in those hungry days when Landlordism was at its worst in this country. Such communion with poverty of a kind different from their own —theirs was only the sort of amateur poverty which people with prospects *enjoy*—added to the development of Mary's character. At this time she must have been endearing and lovable almost beyond even Shelley's powers of expression. She was just twenty years old, and big with child—a time when womanly beauty is at its most awe-inspiring intensity, infolding, brooding, all sensual gesture curbed inward and gripping the fruit of divine lust. Loving-kindness—an abiding quality of her character, in spite of her detachment—

E

was now her crown. Laden with literary work, heavy with her child, responsible for a large household, she yet forgot nothing. The cohorts of the Hunt family descended on them for a large part of the summer; and while this boisterous, untidy crowd was in the house, her baby girl Clara was born. It must have meant a lot of work and domestic thought. Yet we find her adding the following postscript to a deeply affectionate letter to her husband:

'P.S. I wish you would purchase a gown for Milly (the nursemaid), with a little note from Marianne (Mrs Hunt), that it may appear to come from her. You can get one, I should think, for 12/- or 14/-; but it must be *stout*; such a kind of one as we gave to the servant at Bath. Willy has just said good-night to me; he kisses the paper and says good-night to you. Clara is asleep.'

During the autumn Shelley was nearly arrested for debt—Godwin's debts—but the danger was averted and Mary accompanied him on a visit to London. She wanted to renew her friendship with Isabel Baxter, her Dundee friend; but this young lady had married a righteous and elderly man of the name of Booth, who looked upon Shelley with abhorrence and forbade Isabel the company of this wicked atheist and his shameless wife. Mr Booth was evidently a *forceful* man, for even his father-in-law was *forced* to drop the dangerous acquaintance, though this worthy's admiration for Shelley was unbounded and bordered on hero-worship, while he loved Mary like one of his own daughters.

The detractors, however, were growing fat on the delicious spectacle of the atheist with two child-bearing women under his roof, and all his virtue and charity could not allay their resentment. Shelley and his wife realised that Claire's daughter Allegra was likely to become more and more of a social embarrassment to them, and their natural wish was to place the child under the care of her father. That meant taking her out to Italy.

In addition to these Grundian worries, there were

considerations of health. The house at Marlow proved to be dark, cold, and damp; it retarded Mary's recovery after her confinement, while Shelley suffered from frequent indigestion and internal pains, with intermittent fevers—a warning signal of tuberculosis.

In February 1818 they left Marlow, and came to London, where Shelley raised one of his ruinous loans on a post-obit, in order that he might soften the blow of their departure by staving off a few of Godwin's creditors.

For a few weeks the harassed couple enjoyed the company of the London circle. They went to the opera, the museums, and the theatres, and visited and were visited. They saw Keats again, and Shelley was deeply impressed by the noble little figure with his inspired eyes and defiant gesture. Mary saw much of Mary Lamb, who spent the evening with them during their last day in England. Shelley was quite ill by now, however, and his characteristic habit of falling asleep in company was more noticeable than ever. On that last night he suddenly relapsed on a sofa, and so the assembled friends, rather than wake him, went away without bidding him farewell. None of them, except the Hunts, ever saw him again.

SHELLEY and Mary, with Claire, left England together for the third and last time on March 11th 1818. With them now were the three children, William aged two years, Clara aged six months, and Allegra aged one year: no small handful to take abroad in those days. Shelley relieved the trials and tediums of travel by reading Schlegel aloud. With the mercurial physiology of genius, the poet grew better hour by hour as they neared the Mediterranean.

Claire was left at Milan with the children and Elise the nurse, while Shelley and Mary went on to Como for a short holiday. During that time Claire corresponded with Byron, anxious for the future of her child, whom she loved passionately—the first and possibly only deep affection of her life. Byron, however, was shy, bored, and lost to all sense of actuality—so far as women were concerned—by the life of debauchery which he was pursuing in Venice. It was impossible to bring him down to any fixed resolve. At the end of April, however, Allegra left her heart-broken mother, and under the care of Elise went to Byron.

It was all very nerve-racking, and the party wandered up and down in the northern Apennines, seeking to drown their distress in a feast of natural beauty. At last they settled in Leghorn, where Mary made the acquaintance and friendship of Maria Gisborne, who had been a friend of her mother. This lady was the former Mrs Reveley whose hand Godwin had sought too prematurely after her first husband's death. She was still a handsome woman, ' reserved yet with

easy manners ', and a comforting friend to Mary Wollstonecraft's daughter.

News from England of the reception of *Frankenstein* was
encouraging, and Mary, spurred on by her husband's amazing
fertility and enthusiasm, which followed his improvement
in health and happiness, was moved to begin writing again,
in addition to her patient study of Greek, Latin, Italian
and Spanish. Shelley urged her to begin a tragedy for the
stage, and suggested a theme which he afterwards used
himself in *The Cenci*.

The months flew by, winged with eager interests and
labours. Claire, however, was hungering for her child,
and at last Shelley could bear to see her distress no longer.
In August he went to Venice to try to persuade Byron to
agree to some more humane arrangement.

He had not long left Mary, however, when she was beset
by trouble. The excessive heat of the Italian summer was
too much for baby Clara, who fell sick. The anxiety of the
parents, separated as they were, was great, and Shelley
immediately made plans for Mary to travel by easy stages
with the sick child to consult a doctor at Venice. Both
the parents were creatures of the age in their complete lack
of any knowledge of child-welfare.

So now little Clara, sick with diarrhoea and fever, was
jolted and jarred in a conveyance down into the fruity
atmosphere of Venice. Had they stopped at Este, where
Byron had lent them a villa, all might have been well; but
Shelley insisted on pushing on to Venice. He was under
the sway of one of his obsessions, from which nothing could
move him. It was these terrible impulses, a sort of nervous
infatuation with some fixed idea or symbol, that made him,
in spite of his noble generosity and considerateness, so
disastrous to domestic peace and comfort. No woman with
a Martha-disposition would have tolerated him for a moment,
such a menace was he to the niceties and comforts of life.

Mary did not want to go to Venice, which she hated.

Rumour had poisoned her desire to see the place. Their friends the Hoppner's—Hoppner was English consul there —had told her of its social side. She writes to Mrs Gisborne : 'The Hoppners speak with the greatest acrimony of the Italians, and Mr Hoppner says that he was actually driven from Italian society by the young men continually asking him for money. Everything is saleable in Venice, even the wives of the gentry, if you pay well.' But Shelley had the idea that in Venice an efficient doctor might be found. In their hurry they forgot their passports, but after some delay, the customs officers, frightened by Shelley's ghostlike frenzy, allowed them to pass. They took rooms at an inn, and Shelley hurried away in search of a doctor. When he returned Clara was dying and in an hour she succumbed.

Defeated, saddened, they returned to Este, taking Allegra and Claire with them. Byron had been coerced by the combined entreaties of Shelley and Mary, to allow Claire to have her child, during a short holiday at the villa. Trouble and anxiety seemed always to make Shelley productive, and during the fortnight spent at Este, he wrote *Julian and Maddalo*—fruit of renewed intercourse with Byron—and commenced *Prometheus Unbound*. Mary must necessarily have been lonely in her sorrow, for her husband had the solace of composition. She wrote to her father, easing her heart of its pain. Here is his reply: 'I sincerely sympathize with you in the affliction which forms the subject of your letter, and which I may consider as the first severe trial of your constancy and the firmness of your temper that has occurred to you in your life; you should, however, recollect that it is only persons of a very ordinary sort, and of a very pusillanimous disposition, that sink long under a calamity of this nature. I assure you such a recollection will be of great use to you. We seldom indulge long in depression and mourning except when we think secretly that there is something very refined in it, and that it does us honour.'

This return of her sorrow back into the soul where it was engendered resulted in a cold depression—a state of mind which increased almost into a habit as Mary grew older, and as the blows of fate fell faster and crueller. Her mood coloured the family life, and in consequence the whole winter was a sad one for them: a period of sickness, low spirits, and anxiety. Their beloved maid, Elise, by now a friend, was seduced by their Italian man-servant during the winter. He was an obvious rascal, and the Shelleys, in a moment of snobbish conventionality, persuaded the girl to marry him. They regretted it afterwards, for he got his revenge by putting about vile stories of Shelley; how the poet cohabited with Claire, and aided her to procure an abortion. These stories gained such credit, that even the Hoppners believed them. Mary was horror-stricken by their lack of faith, and wrote a noble letter disproving the whole tissue of lies spun by this blackmailing servant. This letter was sent to Byron to forward to the Hoppners. After his death it was found amongst his papers, and much controversy has since arisen as to whether or not he betrayed the trust put upon him. Byron's ragged and top-heavy spirit was probably capable of that act of malice ; but we must remember that to him Shelley was one of the few great men of his generation. He also seriously respected Mary. On the other hand he considered Claire to be capable of any calculated and cold-blooded sensuality—no doubt making her the scapegoat toward his own conscience. What most probably happened is that Byron, realising that there was no other existing copy of the important letter which justified Mary's faith in her husband, made a copy himself, which he forwarded to the Hoppners, while he retained the original.

The winter of 1818–1819 was spent principally between Rome and Naples. The pleasure of travel and the spiritual and mental enjoyment of the treasury of Rome, were clouded partly by their sorrow, and more by a heavy depression which bowed Shelley to the ground. The poems,

In the Euganean Hills and *Stanzas written in Dejection near Naples* are a reflection of this mood. There is a legend that he was mourning over the death of a young married woman whose infatuation for him had made her follow him to Naples, where she died; but it is more probable that his daily responsibilities, his large household, his troubled finances, bad health, and cruel asceticism, all combined to debilitate him and to weaken his nervous hold on life. Mary was jealously distressed, realising that even she could not stimulate him to a new appetite for life. He did not stop work, however, for *Prometheus Unbound* was finished during the winter, while he pursued his studies of philosophy, physics, chemistry, and languages, helping Mary at the same time, and urging her to creative effort. At Rome she discovered a talent for drawing, and often spent whole days at such pleasant work, so much more genial than the misery of literary composition. They found good company, too, in Rome; and thus, with Shelley full of inspiration and persistent in study, together with friendship and the constant joy of the personality of the great city about them, they lingered through the spring into early summer. From week to week their departure to the hills was delayed, though friends warned them of the risks Shelley was running, for he was still far from well. Suddenly little William was stricken with the Roman fever.

He was ill for only a few days, during which the poet sat by his side, not moving for sixty hours. The little boy of three, so lovely in appearance and appealing in his nature, was precious to Shelley; and the horror of this sudden blow from fate penetrated even into the world of Shelley's reality —that hitherto inviolable state. Neither the poet nor his wife make any mention of self-blame for this avoidable disaster. They buried their son in the cemetery, where Keats and Shelley himself were subsequently to lie. Then they fled like wounded creatures, numbed and silent, to the Gisbornes at Leghorn. Mary was crushed. The fact

that she was again with child only added to her grief; for
now she distrusted life. The smiling surface of things was
a malignant lie; and this burden in her womb only another
potential victim for red-clawed chance. Shelley unavailingly
sought consolation by writing *The Cenci*, that single-pulsed
tragedy of vengeance. About this time Mary renewed her
friendship with an art student named Miss Curran, whom
she had known in childhood. The young woman was
talented and gentle-natured, and she proved to be a good
friend, ready with sympathy and tactful help. She had just
made portraits of the Shelleys and their son—and this was
another bond with her. The picture of Shelley, which is
well known, shows him as an oval-faced stag-eyed creature,
totally imcompatible with the ' pardlike spirit, beautiful and
swift ' which we discover in his work. One feels that
El Greco's famous ' St John the Evangelist ' would serve
far more rightly as a portrait of him.

For two months Mary did nothing. She was inconsolable,
and listlessly let the days pass over her head, heedless even of
the troubled lover who was by her side. In the autumn,
however, her wound began to close and she recommenced
her diary and wrote a few letters. October found the family
in Florence, where, on November 12th, 1819, Mary gave
birth to her son, Percy Florence, and broke the spell of
misery.

Apart from the continual irritation caused by the insolent
ingratitude of her step-mother and the concupiscent Godwin,
life passed smoothly. The winter was spent at Pisa, which
became their headquarters during the next few years.
According to the necessities of the seasons, they migrated
to Leghorn and to the baths of San Giuliano, each change
of scene and residence spurring Shelley on to new and
immortal composition. This was his Golden Age, and the
gifts of his genius made him impervious to the minor
troubles of life—finance, scandal, and perfidy of friends.

Claire left them in the Autumn of 1820, obtaining a post

as governess in Florence. Shelley missed her, for he liked
her quick wits and somewhat eloquent emotionalism. Her
mental dishonesty, too, must have been intriguing to his
intensely serious nature. To Mary, however, her absence
was a relief. Mary, herself an enigma by reason of her
nervous aloofness, did not appreciate any equivocal qualities
in another person, especially if that person were a woman
likely to affect the ever-surprising Shelley, whose remote
enthusiasms were liable to sudden raids, infatuations of
light but no heat. Such an occurrence disturbed Mary
profoundly in 1821, while she was occupied with her second
novel, *Valperga*.

At Pisa in the spring of 1821 they encountered the
Greek prince Mavrocordato, a charming hero who figured
later in the Greek insurrection. He much admired Mary and
came every morning to give her lessons in Greek. This was
very stimulating for her, and the attention of the courteous
and scholarly prince did much to restore her natural good
spirits. The next acquaintance, however, was more dis-
turbing. This was a young and aristocratic Italian girl
named Emilia Viviani. Her name is now immortal; for
she inspired Shelley's poem *Epipsychidion*. She was a
beautiful and impressionable young woman, with raven hair
and Greek profile. Her position—she was immured in a
convent by a jealous step-mother—aroused Shelley's compassion. Mary invited the girl to stay with them, and so
an intimacy quickly bound the three people together, more
compactly than was comfortable. Emilia was discovered
to be clever and divinely discontented, as well as beautiful;
and she responded to the eloquence and enthusiasm of the
poet. There was an interchange of letters, enraptured
walks, and fervid conversation. It was unfortunate that
Mary should have to observe the transit of this goddess
just when she herself was at the most dull and mortal moment
of her life with Shelley. She was not so much jealous as
miserably anxious and inferior. She felt that, after all her

effort, faith, and sacrifice, she had failed Shelley. But her depression was premature, for when her husband had worked the infatuation into his magnificent poem, Emilia's purpose was finished.

For awhile life ran more smoothly. Claire was no longer present, and the new infant was thriving. The consequent domestic peace enabled both the poet and his wife to work, and by midsummer Mary had finished her second novel, *Valperga*, a tale of love and intrigue in medieval Florence, when the destinies of lovers were controlled by local politics. Shelley's admiration for his wife was increased by this second book. Alas! it would be hard to find a copy of it nowadays.

Further troubles about Claire and Allegra arose, however, before the summer was far advanced, and Shelley had barely finished and published his elegy of *Adonais*, written as a tribute to the dead John Keats, when he was called to Ravenna by Byron. It was during this absence that Mary wrote her defence of Shelley against the accusations of Paolo, the manservant who had resented their isolated attempt at conforming to convention.

Byron, perplexed by the presence of his beautiful but wilful love-child, had put her into a convent, with the idea of educating her so that she could marry an Italian. Claire was incensed at the proposal, and Shelley's errand was to persuade Byron to some other course of action. He had another purpose also, for his friend Leigh Hunt was in difficulties, and sick with worry. Shelley thereupon acted on a previous suggestion by Byron that the three of them should start a paper in Italy, to be called *The Liberal*. Hunt was written to, and asked to come out to Pisa. Mary, who had always distrusted Byron's favours, was terrified for Hunt's financial safety, and wrote imploring him not to come out. Meanwhile Byron arrived at Pisa with his retinue. He was now a different man. The influence of his mistress, the Countess Guiccioli, had saved him from the rancour and misery of his debaucheries. She was a virtuous, noble-hearted, and highly intelligent girl. She loved him sincerely, for the match was equal. She was rich and of noble birth, and prouder even than her lover. She had, therefore, nothing to gain by her liaison, and it was this fact of her independence that established her influence over the poet. Both Mary and Shelley realized the quality of this rare woman, and enjoyed her friendship.

To complete their circle, three new friends were added during the year. Edward Williams, an ex-army officer, arrived in Pisa with his wife Jane. Jane was a notable beauty, static in temperament, cool and shrewd, yet also warm with a general benevolence which she expressed by a sort of physical rather than a spiritual genius. She was blessed, too, with a lovely singing voice; and this, with her inspired gesture, gave her an entrance into people's very souls, and moved them to an affection which she did not reciprocate. She only *appreciated* it. She was full of candid reserves, and with a limited intelligence could stir greater minds and bring their deeps to light.

Shelley never tired of writing the most passionate poems to her. What artist could have done otherwise from so perfect a model? The movement of her hand, her enigmatic smile that *might* mean so much, the heart-breaking turn of a note in her throat—all these qualities were food to his imagination. He would have played, perhaps, Ferdinand to her Miranda—but she was too full of common sense, and a love of domestic accord. She was fond of her kitchen and a tidy life. This rather disgusted Shelley, but it also kept him safe. Mary was grateful for this and her affection toward Jane was enhanced by the consequent sense of security.

Early in 1822, Edward John Trelawny came to Pisa. Generous, adventurous, and picturesque, he appealed to every member of the party.

As the spring of 1822 advanced, Mary began to feel the heat, for she was again with child. There was also two-year-old Percy Florence, as well as the Williams's babies, to be thought about. Byron's companionship—there was a strong touch of patchouli about his personality—was becoming a little oppressive even to Shelley. Accordingly on February 8th Shelley and Williams went to look for a home by the sea on the Bay of Spezzia, and after several attempts they found a dilapidated house called Casa Magni on the shore at Lerici. The waves washed against the walls.

Before they took up residence in this palatial place, however, death was again to visit the family. While Claire was staying with them on a visit from Florence, information came that her little Allegra had died of typhus in the convent at Bagnacavello. The news was kept from the mother and she was persuaded to accompany the party to Lerici. Shelley hoped that they could bring her gradually to the truth: but a few days after the arrival at Casa Magni, she became suspicious, and Shelley had to tell her. She was distraught, for the child was the one being in the world whom she had truly loved. Byron she called a monster of cruelty, as indeed in this matter he was. She would not be consoled, and insisted on rushing away to try and see her child in its coffin, and to preserve a lock of its hair. She never forgave Byron, and to the end of her long life she cursed his memory.

Casa Magni, lonely, uncomfortable, savagely beautiful, was not a fitting scene for the aftermath of such a bout of nervous misery. Shelley was attacked by nightmares and would run screaming about the house until Mary subdued him by taking him into her breast, as one would take a terrified child. She herself was miserable, ill, and worried: and to be disturbed at night by the waves beating on the walls of the house, and the screams of a vision-haunted genius within, was not healthy for a girl in her condition.

Shelley's overwhelming spiritual fervour, strengthened by his unwearying efforts to attain final consciousness, made his psychic influence abnormal, so that it overflowed the common physical and mental bounds. Even placid Jane Williams was affected, and several times she saw him walking, where indeed it was only an emanation, or a mirage. One day, while in a boat with her and her babies, he proposed that they should capsize the vessel, and ' together solve the great mystery.'

But in between these nervous moods, and the miseries of housekeeping in this superb but comfortless neighbourhood, there were many happy hours.. Mary and Jane, with the children, would wander along the sunlit shore gathering violets and rare shells; while the men would be manœuvring in the bay in the *Ariel*, a boat which had been built for the poet in Genoa.

He would often escape with Mary from the rest of the household, and they would creep along near the shore in a boat and rest for hours rocked by the blue waters, the wife lying with her head on her husband's knees, while he read to her, from their beloved Plato, or Calderon, or the new volume by young Keats, whose *Lamia* so deeply stirred Shelley's admiration. Nature, life, love, caressed them, declaring a momentary truce.

On June 6th, Claire returned, subdued, but strengthened by her grief. Three days later Mary was brought prematurely to bed. From a letter to Mrs Gisborne we learn that for seven hours she lay nearly lifeless. ' At length ice was brought to our solitude; it came before the doctor, so Claire and Jane were afraid of using it; but Shelley overruled them, and by an unsparing application of it, I was restored. They all thought, as did I at one time, that I was about to die.' For a week after the miscarriage she was in great danger, but the combined efforts of the members of the household brought her back to health, though not to serenity. Her spirit was abased, and premonitions of further disaster kept whispering at her heart. The spiritual heaviness into which her bodily lassitude betrayed her, dragged her back from her nearness to Shelley. It was as though she struggled against a fierce tide which was sweeping her away from all that she most cherished. Indeed, the tide was actual: it was the ebbing blood-stream in her veins. Shelley

was at the height of his vital power, highly nervous, tense
with activity, susceptible to every external stimulant and
deterrent. The grand scenery, the beauty and music of
Jane Williams and the discipleship of Williams and Trelawny
—these colourful factors for the moment obscured the weary
Mary. But she was too tired to resent it; even if her deep
faith in her husband's genius would have permitted such
disloyalty. She clung to him, and so clung to life, gradually
building up her strength again. The early summer weeks
passed like an anodyne: music, friendship, and scholarship
nourished her. The quietude was unbroken except for the
gay intrusions of the native Italians, who assembled every
evening on the sands before the house, and danced wildly
to the music of Jane's guitar.

In a letter to Gisborne, Shelley wrote: 'We drive along
this beautiful bay in the evening wind under the summer
moon, until earth appears another world. Jane brings her
guitar and if the past and future could be obliterated the
present would content me so well that I could say with
Faust to the passing moment, " Remain, thou, thou art so
beautiful." '

On July 1st news came from Genoa of the Hunts' departure for Leghorn. Shelley sailed at once to meet them there,
to discover that Marianne was seriously ill, and haunted by
a dread of cancer. Byron's enthusiasm waned when he
learned that the whole Hunt family had arrived to sit on his
doorstep. Any form of respectable and fruitful family life
was repugnant to him; and indeed a less romantic being than
Byron might well have been disgusted by the domestic
complaisance of the Hunts, with their banal optimism and
clannishness, their mutual admiration and bickerings. In
this milieu of the pudding-cloth and the mangle, where
could Childe Harold find balm for his egoism?

These discords had to be resolved, and Shelley was the
only one for the task. After days of strenuous effort he
succeeded, and on July 4th he was able to write to Jane

Williams and to Mary; to the former as a tonic for himself, and to the latter as a task of pity and love. *The Liberal* was to appear with Byron's *Vision of Judgment* in its first number—a guarantee of success. The Hunts were comfortably lodged in Pisa, and a good doctor attendant on Marianne.

Shelley now was free to return home, and on Monday, July 8th, after a morning of shopping and sightseeing with Hunt and Trelawny, he embarked with Edward Williams on the *Ariel*. The sky was not promising, and Trelawny was anxious. As they left the harbour he stood watching the diminishing vessel through his glass, and observed that they were foolishly hugging the shore and that the clouds were massing. Then suddenly the squall broke, and twenty minutes later the horizon was clear. The *Ariel* had vanished. For three days Trelawny searched the shore but nothing came to land.

At Lerici, on that Monday, the women were waiting eagerly for the return of their husbands; but the stormy weather convinced them that the crossing would be deferred. The days passed by, and by Thursday dread had entered Casa Magni. On Friday a letter came from Hunt to Shelley, anxiously enquiring as to their safe passage. It was a cruel way for the truth to be brought.

Mary and Jane at once set out for Pisa, misery urging them on. Byron knew nothing. Although Mary was still an invalid, and had travelled all day, she insisted on continuing the search for news, and at midnight they fled to Leghorn, seeking to escape despair. At Leghorn there was confusion and they were forced to waste the remainder of the night at the wrong inn. They lay down together, in their clothes, until six in the morning. That day's enquiries brought no certainty, and the women decided to return home. Trelawny, a valuable friend in this crisis, accompanied them. Mary was now desperately ill again—but still another week of hopeless hope had to be endured, while Trelawny moved heaven and earth for news, scouring the long reaches of the bay on his horse, questioning the natives for news. News, news, that was the last boon they craved. At last it came; a body had been washed up, a tall figure whose jacket pockets contained a volume of Sophocles, and Keats' last volume folded back at a page of *Hyperion*. The corpse of Williams had been found further up the bay.

Trelawny returned slowly with the news, and the widows sat together waiting. The three humans faced each other for some moments, and then Mary moistened her lips, and asked, ' Is there no hope? ' Trelawny turned and left the room, and a moment later sent in the children.

Mary did not attend the Tuscan funeral rites. Trelawny represented her, and for her snatched Shelley's heart from the flaming pyre.

Jane shortly returned to England; but Mary was too poor. For twelve months she remained in Italy; torturing herself with Italy as a relic of the dead; turning to Italy as a suicide turns to death. Byron tried to help her, but grew tired of her grief and indecision. For the remainder of her time, she, with her fatherless boy, stayed with the Hunts, who surrounded her with noisy but not too comprehending sympathy. Leigh Hunt himself, however, understood her grief, and shared it, for he had worshipped at the same shrine. Their friendship was confirmed for life.

F

II

THE EBB-TIDE

THE year which Mary spent in Italy following her loss, seemed to act as an anæsthetic; and it was not until she returned to England after an absence of five years that the full agony of her grief overwhelmed her. She returned to a sordid anticlimax. Now that the dream was broken, she found herself in a muddle of financial and legal quibbling about her own, her son's and her father's affairs. The Shelley family treated her as a common adventuress and shut her out absolutely, save for a grudging and insulting pittance from the petty-minded Sir Timothy. She found new people, new manners, and a cool indifference wherever she went. The conservative England with its jealous and prudent skies, its distrust of the sun, gathered round her like an impersonal code of rules, like a mechanical institution. She shrank into her shell, morbid, depressed, and unhealthily humiliated. Not even her growing literary reputation could dispel her sense of inferiority, for she had never quite believed in herself, and she now felt that a world which praised her and remained indifferent to the work of Shelley was a world out of proportion and therefore valueless.

Shelley with his insatiable greed for sympathy and comprehension had drained away her vitality. Giving her so much, lifting her up to a giddy intellectual and spiritual virtuosity, he had at the same time made terrible exactions. Nobody could understand Mrs Shelley's loss, and thenceforth people began to look upon her sorrow as a form of gentle valetudinarianism, and to treat her as an invalid, beautiful, brilliant, wistful, whose mysterious detachment gave the stimulus of uncertainty and a charming discomfort to her generous companionship. To the last moment of her life, she brooded over those few years of transfiguration, preserving and worshipping in her heart the ghost who had inspired her, torturing herself with a long-continued examination of her passion, and finding in it, belatedly, defects that set up an ecstasy of remorse.

Life, however, would not permit her the indulgence of such child-like clinging to the mother-skirts of the past, and for her own and her son's interests she was forced to return to England.

Her father met her on August 25th, 1823, as she landed, and he took her and her infant son Percy Florence to his house in the Strand. She found, to her rather wan satisfaction, that a dramatic version of *Frankenstein* was having a successful run at the English Opera House, and that her father had arranged for a new edition of the novel. Distrusting the commercial value of her literary capabilities, however, she approached her father-in-law, Sir Timothy, and so began the long, weary, and humiliating course of negotiations with Sir Timothy's solicitor which lasted until the old baronet's death in 1844 at the age of ninety.

She was given a small income of £100 a year, with the threat that if she published a life of her husband the allowance would cease. Sir Timothy never lost the idea that his son was an unsavoury reprobate, whose name and infamy it was his duty as head of the family to suppress as far as possible. Mary published Shelley's *Posthumous Poems* in 1824. The book would have had a portrait of the poet had it not been for Jane Williams, who had mislaid the original sketch. This lovely, musical, indolent woman had a singular lack of continuity in her make-up. She lived in the joy and pain of the present; and the past with its loyalties and memories had little hold upon her. Mary clung to her because she was so inextricably a part of that past. But Jane seemed indifferent to, and a little incredulous—perhaps rightly—of Mary's attachment to her.

The result of the publication of the *Poems* was a few lukewarm reviews, and violent action from Sir Timothy, who threatened that if the unsold remainder of the edition was not recalled he would stop all further allowance to Mary and her son. He also demanded that all of Shelley's manuscripts should be placed in the custody of a third party. As this party was her friend Peacock, and as she anticipated that Sir Timothy would not live long to frustrate the growth of her husband's fame, Mary complied.

It was necessary now for her to add to her allowance, for she needed money to educate her boy. She therefore published her second novel, *Valperga*, written during the last years of Shelley's life. This she followed up with another, *The Last Man*, which appeared in 1826. It is a highly fanciful story of the annihilation of the human race by plague, with only the hero, Adrian, surviving. Adrian is an obvious pen-portrait of Shelley.

Although published anonymously Mary's work was recognized, and the reviewers mentioned her name in the critiques. Sir Timothy again descended, and stopped her allowance.

In September of that year, however, Shelley's son Charles —by Harriet—died of consumption, and little Percy Florence became heir to the estate. Sir Timothy was forced to be more gracious, and while he still refused to receive Mary he made her an allowance of £250, to be increased the following year to £300.

Working against her backward-looking sorrow was Mary's love of companionship and social life, and as time cicatrized her wound, she naturally developed this side of her personality. Established in a modest house, she quietly accumulated round her much of the literary and intellectual life of London. Not only her own charm and power but also the prestige of her parents and the romantic connection with Shelley made her a centre of attraction to the rising generation of writers, whom she added to her circle of friends from the past. At her little house in Somerset Street, Portman Square, she gave ' at homes ' where such people as Bulwer Lytton, Lord Dillon, Barry Cornwall, Praed, the Cowden Clarkes, and Vincent Novello and others would gather to have talk and music, or to listen to the spell-binder, Tom Moore, sing his pretty tinsel songs with such incomparable charm that both he and his audience would fall a-weeping.

One of Mary's greatest admirers at this time was Mary Victoria Novello, who afterwards became the wife of Charles Cowden Clarke, the early friend of John Keats. Mary Novello was a girl of sixteen at the time she wrote the following description of the distinguished and beautiful authoress of the now famous *Frankenstein*:

' Her well-shaped, golden-hair head, almost always a little bent and drooping; her marble white shoulders and arms statuesquely visible in the perfectly plain black velvet dress, which the customs of that time allowed to be cut low and which her own taste adopted (for neither she nor her sister in sorrow ever wore the conventional " widow's weeds " and " widow's cap "); her thoughtful, earnest eyes; her short upper lip and intellectually curved mouth, with a certain close-compressed and decisive expression while she listened and a relaxation into fuller redness and mobility when speaking; her exquisitely formed white, dimpled, small hands, with rosy palms and plumply commencing fingers that tapered into tips as slender and delicate as those in a Vandyke portrait.'

Amid all this popularity, however, she clung with intensity to the people who had known her in her life with Shelley, and as one by one they fell away, she closed the doors of herself upon herself, becoming a little more enigmatic with each such gesture of self-protection. In 1824 Byron died, and she received the news sadly, although Byron's outburst

of savagery against her, when she had shown such indecision
at Genoa the previous year, had destroyed her affection for
him.   Indeed, it is doubtful if she ever had any; for she had
been rather hypnotized than attracted by him, even during
the intimacy at Diodati, when he had treated her with a
respect and friendship such as he gave no woman, except his
half-sister Augusta Leigh, and his mistress, the Countess
Guiccioli.

There remained four people, who, since they had known
Shelley and had shared in the tragedy at Lerici, were sacred
to Mary.   They were her step-sister Claire, Leigh Hunt,
Trelawny, and Jane Williams.   Claire, who was to receive
a legacy of £12,000 under Shelley's will, had to earn her
living until Sir Timothy died and she could inherit her
property.   She obtained various posts as companion, or
governess, mainly in Russia, and punctuated her bizarre
viscissitudes with her witty letters.   Mary saw little of her,
and towards the end found her irrepressible spirits too much
of a burden.   During her last visit, when Mary was living
at Field Place with Percy, who had succeeded to the title,
Claire had to be asked to leave, and Mary saw no more of
the woman who, in her own words ' has been the bane of my
life since I was three years old.'   Claire survived her by
twenty-seven years, dying at Florence in 1878.

With Leigh Hunt and his menagerie of a household Mary
was always comfortable.   Their happy-go-lucky untidiness
provided an antidote to her own slight tendency to succumb
to an old-maidish preciseness.   The house teemed with
young life, immediate troubles, illnesses, and enthusiastic
schemes of literary and financial regeneration.   Leigh Hunt's
golden-hearted character, with its occasional touches of
amiable slipperiness, rode the storms serenely.   Mary helped
him by indefatigable literary labours, and by a late-developed
faculty of dealing with printers, publishers, and other author-
ities who refuse to make allowances for ' temperament.'
She straightened out the tangles in the affairs of *The Examiner*,

the great liberal paper in the days before Liberalism became Nonconformist, Free Trade, and pot-hatted.

When Mary returned to England, her first wish was to be with Jane Williams again. How far she loved Jane for her own sake it is difficult to determine, so interwoven was her affection with that greed which sorrow shows for hoarding up recollections and mementoes of its origin. Jane was the most vivid reminder that Mary possessed. They had sat side by side when Leigh Hunt's letter arrived ; they had shared those hours of torture in the inn at Leghorn; they had waited in Casa Magni for the sound of Trelawny's horse as he came with hope broken in his hands. And also, Jane had had a subtle attraction for Shelley which she, by her calm sagacity and detachment, had kept at a steady equilibrium. With any other woman, at that time when Mary's attraction for him had been at a temporary ebb, he might have plunged deeply, moved by one of his insane impulses. Mary must never have forgotten that, nor have ceased to be grateful to Jane, the intoxicating Miranda who had such a cool head and heart.

Mary came to England to find Hogg deeply in love with her friend. Hogg's affectation of cynical legalism was no more than a gesture of his romantic and even sentimental nature. People, rather than causes, attracted or repelled him, and he was either in love with a woman or gently hostile to her. His actions were guided by a sensuous kindness, and therefore he could show his self-styled cynicism only in relation to absent friends. Face to face, their looks, tone of voice, personal aura, moved him as a stage-piece will move an adolescent, and he crumbled into good nature. Even toward Shelley, the passion of his youth, and his life-long adoration, he could in recollection profess an amused detachment which only veiled his feminine tenderness. Jane Williams' impersonal kindness, her lovely voice, and person ever in repose, her semi-sincere charm always withdrawing itself, cat-like, from the embrace of friends and lover, all these opposites attracted him. It was five years before his suit was successful, for Jane had been deeply attached to her husband, while the circumstances of his death, together with the example set by Mary, made her ambitious to maintain the luxury of a sorrow that it was not in her nature to feel. In 1827 she accepted Hogg and they made a very happy marriage. Perhaps as a reaction from her years of strenuous grief under Mary's monitorship, she indiscreetly talked, soon after her marriage, about the days at Lerici, and threw hints abroad that Mary had, with good cause, been jealous of her. Naturally the stories came to Mary's ears. It was a terrible blow to her, for the impulsive girl had put all her faith in her friend.

She did her best to conquer the resentment, and wrote a noble letter to Jane that would have moved the coldest heart. The bonds between them were too strong to be broken, and the wound was hidden. The old intimacy was gone, however, and gradually Mrs Hogg became more and more removed as the cares of marriage absorbed her.

The fourth member of Mary's intimate circle, Trelawny, was a never-failing solace to her. This great figure of a man, who combined in one person qualities from half the characters in the Iliad, treated Mary as a comrade, a sister, and a lover-in-absence. He wrote her long letters from all the odd corners of Europe, consoling her, abusing her, leaning on her as a son, and caressing her with a fierce tenderness. He confided the MSS. of his now famous *Recollections of a Younger Son* to her for excision and publication, leaving her to make what terms she could. He sent one of his illegitimate children to be educated in England, and told Mary to keep an eye on the girl. He asked her to collaborate with him in a Life of Shelley, and Mary had some little difficulty in extricating herself from the alarming project. It is a pity that he did not write it, for the little that he gives us about Shelley in the *Recollections* shows that he rightly saw the poet without sentimentalizing about him. He recognized Shelley's fierce, devastating intellectual strength, and the supple will that directed it. He saw in Shelley a man stronger and more independent than himself.

Toward the end of 1828 he proposed to come to England to see Mary, and she faintly dreaded the meeting, for earlier in the year fate had dealt her a typically cruel stroke. In July she had gone for a holiday to Paris, her first trip abroad since leaving Italy. She no sooner arrived than she fell ill with small-pox. The preparations which had been made to honour the authoress went for nothing. She says that ' the Parisians were very amiable, and, a monster to look at as I was, I tried to be agreeable, to compensate to them.'

It was many years before she recovered her beauty. Though not pitted, a sort of dimness settled over her complexion and her glorious hair lost its lustre. Trelawny, writing about his return, was very tender, ending his letters with such phrases as ' You are my dear and long true friend, and as such I love you.' Though she was brave about her loss—as evidenced by pathetic half-humorous references to the novelty of plainness—she must have dreaded the effect of her altered appearance on Trelawny's spectacular mind. He was not disturbed, however, and two years later, following her great efforts as midwife to his book, he proposed as follows:

' I should not wonder if fate, without our choice, united us ; and who can control his fate? I blindly follow his decrees, dear Mary.'

To which she replied :

' Never—neither you nor anybody else. Mary Shelley shall be written on my tomb—and why? I cannot tell, except that it is so pretty a name that though I were to preach to myself for years, I never should have the heart to get rid of it. My name will never be Trelawny. I am not so young as I was when you first knew me, but I am as proud. I must have the entire affection, devotion, and above all, the solicitous protection of any one who would win me. You belong to womenkind in general, and Mary S. will never be yours.'

Their friendship continued unbroken to the end of her life.

She continued to devote herself to her son, and to her literary work. Very little of the latter has survived the criticism of Time, for the reason that it was all no more than variations on a single spiritual theme. *Frankenstein*, inspired by her contact with Shelley and Byron during the memorable holiday on the lake of Geneva, is the only book which has won a permanent place in English fiction. During her life, however, each succeeding book added to her popularity and financial competence. She was able to send her son to Harrow and to maintain her father up to the last few years of his long life, when he was given a sinecure Government post as a recognition of his contribution to English political philosophy. He died in 1836 and was buried with Mary Wollstonecraft in St Pancras Churchyard, the first trysting place of Mary and Shelley.

For four years after her father's death Mary worked steadily with her pen, principally upon a long series of biographies of Italian and Spanish poets for *Lardner's Cyclopædia*.

In 1841 her son came of age and his grandfather gave him an allowance of £400 a year. This enabled mother and son to indulge in the long-cherished dream of an extended tour on the Continent, which resulted in a travel book, *Rambles in Germany and Italy*. After an absence of over twenty years, she visited Geneva again, the scene of her happiest moments, when youth, love, and genius combined to enrich her. She saw the scene now through eyes that were heavy with disillusion and that tragic tameness which comes from a loss of hope. This is how she describes the return :

' The far Alps were hid, the wide lake looked drear. At length I caught a glimpse of the scenes amongst which I had lived, when first I stepped out from childhood into life. There on the shores of Bellerive stood Diodati; and our humble dwelling, Maison Chapuis, nestled close to the lake below. There were the terraces, the vineyards, the upward path threading them, the little port where our boat lay moored. I could mark and recognize a thousand peculiarities, familiar objects then, forgotten since—now replete with recollections and associations. Was I the same person who had lived there, the companion of the dead—for all were gone? Even my young child, whom I had looked upon as the joy of future years, had died in infancy. Not one hope, then in fair bud, had opened in maturity; storm and blight and death had passed over, and destroyed all. While yet very young, I had reached the position of an aged person, driven back on memory for companionship with the beloved, and now I looked on the inanimate that had surrounded me, which survived the same in aspect as then, to feel that all my life since is an unreal phantasmagoria—the shades that gathered round that scene were the realities, the substances and truth of the soul's life which I shall, I trust, hereafter rejoin.'

In April 1844, ' Old Time,' as Mary had nicknamed the obstinately long-lived Sir Timothy, died, and her son succeeded to the baronetcy and to what remained of the estate. Shortly after this he married happily, both for himself and his mother. Mary's struggles were over, and in the calm that followed, she realized that she was worn out. She sat in the sun of peace and solicitude, tended by her beloved son and daughter. Gradually the brave heart slowed down and she died on February 21st, 1851, after an epilogue which had lasted for twenty-nine years.

BIBLIOGRAPHY

E. J. TRELAWNY. Recollections, Records, and Letters.

E. E. WILLIAMS. Diary.

MRS ANGELI. Shelley and his Friends in Italy.

LUCY MADOX ROSSETTI. Mary Shelley (Eminent Women Series).

MRS MARSHALL. Mary Wollstonecraft Shelley. (2 Vols.)

ROGER INGPEN. Shelley in England.

ROGER INGPEN (ED.). Shelley's Works (Julian Edition).

WM. M. ROSSETTI. Memoir on Shelley.

MRS CAMPBELL. Shelley and the Unromantics.

BOOKS BY MARY SHELLEY

Frankenstein (1818).

Valperga, or The Life and Adventures of Castruccio, Prince of Lucca (1823).

The Last Man (1826).

The Fortunes of Perkin Warbeck (1830).

Lodore (1835).

Falkner (1837).

Journal of a Six Weeks' Tour.

Rambles in Germany and Italy (1840–43).

Edition of Shelley's Works, with Notes (1838).

Part of the first chapter, giving a resumé of the life of Mary Wollstonecraft, the mother of Mary Shelley, appeared in an article in the "Spectator." The author has to thank the Editor for permission to use that material.

REPRESENTATIVE
WOMEN

∽ R E P R E S E N T A T I V E   W O M E N ∽
General Editor : Francis Birrell

∽

THERE is an idea abroad, sedulously fostered by the newspapers, that women after centuries of claustration are at last coming into their own; and that never before in the world's history have they been able to show the smallest portion of their worth. It is the object of the series entitled 'Representative Women' to dispel this comfortable generalization and to prove to the adorable adepts of our night clubs that there is a standard up to which they should at any rate attempt to live.

The series will give in biographical form a picture of female accomplishment throughout the ages. It has been thought better to concentrate on women eminent in private life rather than on those public personages, like Queen Elizabeth, who could hardly be dealt with adequately in an essay of twenty-five thousand words, or on artists, like Miss Austen, who are fully revealed in their art. Persons so placed or gifted are often the less typical of their age and milieu. With these exceptions, women of all types and ages will be included among the early subjects. By the time the series is complete, a catena of female achievement will have been forged. The authors will show that no period in the world's history has lacked women of energy and character able to leave a mark on their times.

✍ REPRESENTATIVE WOMEN ✍

Each writer has been chosen for his intimate knowledge of his subject, and the treatment will be as various as the persons treated. No attempt will be made by the editor to stereotype a point of view.

Among early contributors to the series will be :

> MARTIN ARMSTRONG
>
> CLIFFORD BAX
>
> FRANCIS BIRRELL
>
> RICHARD CHURCH
>
> BONAMY DOBRÉE
>
> WILLA MUIR
>
> ARTHUR WALEY
>
> V. SACKVILLE WEST

and other well known writers.